THEREBY HANGS A TALE

By the same author:
The Hawk and the Dove
The Wounds of God
The Long Fall

Thereby Hangs a Tale

PENELOPE WILCOCK

KINGSWAY PUBLICATIONS
EASTBOURNE

ISBN 0 85476 399 6

Produced by Bookprint Creative Services
P.O. Box 827, BN21 3YJ England for
KINGSWAY PUBLICATIONS LTD
Lottbridge Drove, Eastbourne, E Sussex BN23 6NT.
Printed in Great Britain

For my friend
Giles Goddard
to whom I owe so much:
thank you, Giles.
With my love.

Contents

Acknowledgements

This book was four years in the researching and writing, and a lot of growth and change happened in that time, which is reflected in these stories and accompanying notes. Growth and change happen as a result of insight, and insight happens through interaction with other people. These stories would never have been written without the insights, growth and change that were brought about by the friends and companions on the journey who shared their lives with me over these four years.

So I want to say thank you, especially to the following people:

John Kennedy, whose Poverty Project sparked me off in the first place, in the task of communicating to the church the themes of these stories.

Our street sweeper, whose name I do not know, for taking the time to drink tea with me and talk about his life and work and family.

The men of Northeye Prison Tuesday Night Fellowship, whose loving acceptance, humour and honesty made a profound impression on me; and the Revd Gordon Chambers, who enabled that fellowship to be a place of welcome, healing and kindness.

The staff and clients of the HUCAC snack bar, especially John and June Turner, whose utter commitment to the gospel humbles me.

The staff and students of the Southwark Ordination Course, who have from time to time prevented me from totally disintegrating; especially Giles, who spent hours talking in the pub, and helped me produce a respectable manuscript.

The congregations of the Hastings, Bexhill and Rye Methodist Circuit, on whom these stories were tried out.

Mark and Gill Barrett and my husband Roger for listening and encouraging.

To all of these people, a most heartfelt thank you. As well as enabling me to write this book, you have shaped my thinking, and changed my life, and helped me to discover a vision of a God who is full of mercy; a God whose face is kind, and who is to be trusted.

Introduction

Story-telling as germs

I wonder if you have come across a sentence like this in a story-book: 'Samantha told Eric about the bank robbers who had made their million and were now living in comfortable exile: and the germ of an idea began to grow in Eric's mind.'

The germ of an idea. About twenty-five years ago, when yoghourt was an unknown and exotic food imported to this island from Europe (adapted to a British palate by the addition of much food colouring and sugar) and the pronunciation of the word 'muesli' was charming in its eccentric diversity, there was a vogue for eating wheatgerm. Wheatgerm was promoted as good for you, contributing to long life and wellbeing, because it is a *live* food. It is the bit of the wheat that makes the grain grow into a new plant. It holds the genetic information and the squirt of magic that makes everything happen when the seed falls into the ground and dies.

If you carefully divide a peanut in half you will see a tiny object that is in fact two miniscule seed leaves; this tiny object is the germ of the nut. The main bit of the nut is the starchy food store from which this germ will draw

11

nourishment as it grows into a new nut plant. And that tiny thing contains the genetic information on which the responsibility for a whole forest may depend: because it is the germ of an idea; it carries within its tiny, frail structure the idea of the plant.

If you have ever watched one of those absorbing television documentaries about genetics, where scientists explain how sperm and ova unite and grow from there into a mature human being, you may, like me, have been fascinated to notice that the scientists, in explaining the genetic process, cannot get away from the language of story-telling. The DNA, the wonderful, mysterious double helix of genetic material, contains they say, information, a message. In other words, the genetic material, whether of a human embryo, the germ of a grain of wheat, or the miniature leafy thing concealed in the peanut, is a story. We begin as stories, as the germ of an idea. The story of what we are, of our destiny, is hidden in every cell of our being and determines what we will become.

All life proceeds from stories. This concept was intuitively understood by the writer of John's Gospel, long ago, who knew nothing about DNA and genetics, but who had the wisdom to begin his beautiful prologue: 'In the beginning was the Word.'

And even more thousands of years ago, the writer of Genesis tells us: 'The earth was a formless void, there was darkness over the deep, and God's spirit hovered over the water. God said, "Let there be light," and there was light.'

Life is *called* into being; thought, breath, form, movement, relationship, growth cannot begin without the speaking of the words of life.

Genes. Chromosomes. The story of what I am, the germ of the idea of me. The message without which my life cannot begin.

Words and ideas

It is by language that we begin to think. A sad way of learning this lesson has been the realisation that some deaf people, those who were deprived of both hearing language and sign language, lacked the tools of conceptual thought. They were not 'simple', not intellectually deficient, but until they had language, the world of ideas remained closed to them. Only when they were introduced to communication and language by sign, did conceptual, abstract thinking dawn into their lives, previously confined to the poverty of concrete and mundane experiences, and feelings without the expression of flow of thought.

It is hard for us to grasp the fact that, because of the way our brains work—because of the very way life is designed—language precedes thought, not the other way round. We may have an idea, and then struggle to express it; in that sense the idea comes first and articulating it comes second, but what we often don't realise is that we would never have the idea in the first place without a word-seed dropped into our minds.

What a complicated notion! Perhaps an example will serve to explain, but hold on to your hat because this is controversial ground. Inclusive language. Has the controversy about inclusive language hit your church?

Exclusive language talks like this:

. . . *us men and our salvation* . . .

. . . *when a man is in Christ he is a new creation* . . .

. . . *Brothers, this Lord Jesus shall return again* . . .

. . . *peace on earth, goodwill to all men* . . .

Long ago, when our language developed, women did not enjoy the social status they do today. They used to be thought to have no souls. They were the property of their fathers, and upon marrying became the property of their husbands. Their things were not their own, but belonged to

their husbands or fathers, so they could not inherit anything. That is why when a woman married she took her
husband's name, because without him she was nothing:
she was, quite literally, his property. She was there to 'love,
honour and obey' him, to bear and raise his children, keep
his house and serve him. Still today, an orthodox Jew will
in his daily prayers thank God he was not born a woman.
Still today a married woman is usually known as 'Mrs John
Smith', anonymously bearing her husband's name.

Now, because in history women were soul-less chattels,
they did not feature in the language as it grew up. As
English developed, it developed referring to people as
'men', because in the early days, men were the only
people worth mentioning; women had no vote, no say,
no influence.

Times have changed, but sometimes women express
frustration that still they feel like second-class citizens. In
the very traditional world of the Christian church, they
often are still second-class citizens; there to listen, serve
and obey.

Some people like to keep things that way, believing this
to be the biblical pattern laid down for human society for
all ages. Others have a different understanding of the
gospel, and would like to see women and men enjoying
equality in everything. The secret of changing or staying as
we are lies in our language: chairman, manhole cover,
mankind. In our language, women do not exist. In our
language women are invisible.

At first, when this is said, people laugh and mock.
'Personhole cover!' they say, and it makes them laugh.
When they think about changing 'mankind' to 'woman-
kind', it even makes them angry. They say, 'But when I say
"men", I don't mean males, I mean women as well—it's an
inclusive term!' They say that God has within the divine
nature both masculinity and femininity—that female and

male humanity was made in God's image—and yet the idea of 'Mother God' provokes outrage.

This is because culture and tradition have a really powerful emotional hold on us, and in our culture and tradition, women are linguistically absent. The *idea* of woman is absent from the English language, and as long as it is, women will continue to be inferior to men in our society. Language precedes concept, not the other way round, in the working of the human brain.

A friend of mine recently reported the experience of listening to the Archbishop of Canterbury conducting worship on the radio. She said that as she listened, she found herself with a sense of being wanted, being part of the worship, being loved. Puzzled about why this should be so, she paid closer attention to what he was saying, and realised that he was using inclusive language; that he was talking about brothers and sisters, women and men, being careful to make women linguistically visible in the words he used.

That is why one cannot sell the notion of inclusive language to people who never use it. Like deaf people who have not experienced speech, the idea has never flowered in their minds; because it is not until they have experienced inclusive language that they will be enabled to experience inclusive thought. Until then, it will be, quite literally, non-sense to them.

It was not that God saw the light and said, 'Ah! Light!' but that God said, 'Let there be light,' and there was light. That is how it is with us; we are the creatures of the creative Word.

The sense of cultural alienation in some women because of exclusive language, and the complete bafflement in others as to why they should feel like that, is one sad example of the way words, language, carry the germs of thought. But that is only one example.

When Jesus taught about the kingdom of God, he taught

by dropping word-germs into people's minds (we usually call them parables). 'The kingdom of heaven is like this . . . and like this . . . and like this . . .' He built up a story bank for them. Without explaining or giving complicated philosophical analyses, he allowed the stories, seeds of the concept that fired him, to drop into the minds of his hearers. There they would develop into a mature understanding, firmly and organically cultured in the mind of the individual, so that the idea was their own idea— positively grasped, not tenuously remembered. And of course, his stories were accessible to everyone: educated and illiterate, old and young.

Interestingly enough, since the subject of inclusive language has been raised, have you noticed how unusually visible women are in the stories of Jesus?

The kingdom of heaven is like a woman who lost a silver coin . . .

The kingdom of heaven is like a woman making bread . . .

There were ten wise girls and ten foolish girls . . .

Thank you, Jesus.

A gospel for everybody?

In my lifetime of churchgoing, I have noticed that some people never seem to stick—some *kinds* of people. The people who come to church seem to be all more or less the same type. In recent years as churchgoing declines more and more, worried congregations lay on missions and outreach programmes to try and persuade people to see the light and become like us, and attend church. It doesn't seem to be working.

I remember reading as a young child a story about a beautiful princess whose jealous father didn't want her to get married. What he did was to build a smooth, slippery glass mountain, sit her on the top, and send out an edict to say, 'Here she is. If you can get her, you can have her.'

Many suitors came with high hopes, and they did want her, long for her, but one after another they all failed. Nobody stopped them. In fact they were encouraged to come. But the glass mountain was too slippery for them. Nobody needed to prevent them—they slid off it by themselves.

On Sunday morning, where are the black people and the people with physical disabilities? Where are the homeless people? Where are the builders' labourers? Where are the teenagers? Where are the gay people? Where are the mentally ill people and the mentally handicapped people? I don't know where they are, but they're not in our church, or not in any significant numbers. Why not? Are there bouncers at the door to keep them out? Not at all. Everyone is welcome, or so we always say. We sit at the top of the glass mountain and we say that everyone is welcome, and we wonder why they never come.

The night outside

Some of us live very safe lives: law-abiding, more or less content, reasonably financially secure, in families or groups of friends that rub along well enough together. When our lives are like that, people whose lives are characterised by crime, abuse, misery, violence, forsakenness, debt, drugs, mental instability, can seem very threatening, a breath of the night outside, endangering the safety of our well-lit world; a cold shadow disturbing the comfort of the living room.

Although the gospels speak a great deal about freedom and peace—about love and release—it does not take much looking for an observer to notice that fear has more than a foothold in the outlook of the average church congregation. The intrusion of a drunken man into a service can 'ruin the worship'. The contemplation of homosexual love can provoke a reaction almost hysterical, beyond all reasonable moral judgement. An ex-prisoner joining a congregation can find himself alone in a little pool of space in even the most crowded church. Fear.

We fear the unknown, the darkness, the other. We fear those whose lives are out of control, those who see things differently from us, those for whom everything is disintegrating. And yet, the gospel might be summed up in those words Jesus said so often: 'Don't be afraid. It's me.'

This is not another guilt trip. This is not an invitation to lay on more reform programmes for fallen humanity. It is an invitation to look at some of the people who make us afraid, and think again.

When we read the gospel stories, we like to identify ourselves with the disciples. But really, the group most closely parallel with the churchgoers of today are the Pharisees. They were the honest, faithful, Godfearing believers who took their religion seriously, worshipping regularly and living according to their faith. Jesus once went for dinner with one of these good men, a man called Simon, who had heard Jesus was a prophet and wanted (very prudently) to see for himself. During dinner, a prostitute gatecrashed the party, and draped herself all over Jesus' legs, crying and stroking him and behaving in a very socially inappropriate fashion. The Pharisee, quite reasonably, thought that this was an opportunity for Jesus to use his prophetic gift to discern the unsavoury nature of the woman's profession and call her to repentance.

'Simon,' Jesus said to the man (he called him by his name; I called him 'the Pharisee', but Jesus addressed him as a person), 'do you see this woman?'

And that is the question that reverberates down the centuries of history. 'Do you see this woman?'

Because it is when the people of the darkness outside are seen not as 'thieves', 'drug-abusers', 'homosexuals', 'mentally handicapped', but for the real, vulnerable, beautiful human beings they are that the darkness ceases to be frightening.

This book has been written so that the church can pause and ask: 'Where are they, these people who never come? Where are they? Who are they? What will they do to us if we dare to climb down the glass mountain and risk the real world for a change?'

In each of these stories, we look at the people the church has shut out in an effort to keep life smooth and easy. We consider the implications of the fact that everywhere people are finding their way to God, not because of the church but in spite of the church, that God speaks to people on the street and by the sea and in the kitchen—wherever they are. We remember that sometimes people whose lives we condemn have more to teach us of the gospel than we have to teach them.

Telling stories

Another reason for this book is that after some years of preaching sermons, I realised that virtually nobody, including myself, could remember the content of any sermon at all. Preachers like me were preaching their hearts out on a Sunday morning, covering an impressive range of theological and biblical material, and still the cry went up, 'Why don't we ever get any *teaching* in this church?'

So, reflecting that people are literally, physically made up of stories, and that an idea cannot take root in the human mind until it is carried there by words, I tried a new approach. I tried the approach of Jesus, who only ever taught the people with stories.

The stories are the germs of ideas, of concepts: concepts of an open and inclusive church, not a virginal princess crouching at the top of a glass mountain. Concepts of a God who listens; who is tender and passionate, full of mercy and grace.

The stories introduce various theological themes and issues, because it is my experience that whereas people are often alarmed at discussing theology if it is presented in the form of abstract ideas, they can take those same ideas on board quite comfortably when they are presented in story form. This way they come to 'own' the idea more readily, assimilating the concept naturally instead of grappling with it as an alien force. The cerebral doorway is not the only way in to theology, and ordinary people have for too long been disempowered by theological ideas being presented primarily in abstruse sermons and extra-ordinarily boring textbooks. The smallest child can grasp the profoundest concept if it is communicated in a story; and that is the way to learn to love ideas.

To help you to find your way around this book and choose the stories most suitable for your group, here are some pointers.

There are eight short stories, and then three much shorter pieces. This gives you some flexibility in finding an appropriate piece for a particular occasion.

1. The first story, *In Grosvenor Street*, is about a street sweeper. Our lives are thronged with people (ticket inspectors, lavatory attendants, office cleaners, refuse collectors, postmen, window cleaners) who have dealings with us and yet we know nothing about them. It is not a good thing that our lives be characterised by anonymity. It is important to bear in mind with everyone we meet that this is a *person*, with likes and dislikes, memories, sadness and dreams and hopes. We should keep enough space in our lives to respond to people as people, and remember that how we are with them witnesses to the God we believe in (yes it does, even if we never say a word to them about God). So this story is about a street sweeper, to remind us to think of public service officials as *people*, not just as part of the background.

The theological theme explored in *In Grosvenor Street* is

the humanity of Jesus. In the worship of the church we exalt and praise Jesus as Lord and King, but he can be lost to us as Friend and Brother unless we stop to consider his humanity from time to time.

2. Next is the story *Time to Put Things Right*. The central character of this story is the hidden person many of us carry inside: the person trapped unhappily and struggling inadequately in a conventional lifestyle, whose principal deep-seated emotions are resentment and shame.

The theological theme explored is that of finding healing and forgiveness in sacramental relationships; when other people can be for us the touching place with the unseen God. Trust is a central issue in this story.

3. The next story in the book is *Release*, and in this story the outsider in the spotlight is a young man newly released from prison; raw, defensive and thoroughly unacceptable to his sister's house group, to which he pays a most unwelcome visit. The story invites us to ponder how we ourselves cope with those who mess up the way we like things done, and threaten our securities.

The theological theme concerns freedom and imprisonment, and you may like to use it to consider the straitjacket of religion and the freedom of the Spirit of God.

4. After that is *The Perfect Host*. In this story we follow the experiences of a teenager whose girlfriend has just ditched him. The young man's background is one of poverty, his mother struggling to bring up a family singlehanded after the father of the family leaves. The sadnesses of the young man's life compound into misery, and in the story he finds something to hold onto in the crucifixion of Jesus, and in the meaning his own sufferings receive in the remembrance of the death of Jesus in the Lord's Supper.

Theologically, this story explores what is happening when we celebrate the Eucharist, and links it with our everyday experiences of brokenness and suffering.

5. *A Dream Come True* is not an easy story for a Christian

group to consider, because it offers no comfortable answers and no happy ending. It is the story of two prisoners, one a cynic and an atheist, the other a believer whose approach to life is wildly unrealistic, reflecting the damage of years of abuse and neglect. There is a third, unseen character in the story, and that is the absent church. The church that lives in a totally different world from the two men in the story, and therefore has nothing to offer either of them in time of crisis. During their time in prison, the atheist of the pair is the one who fulfils the loving, listening role that represents the presence of God. He is the son who refused to work in the vineyard when his father asked him, but then went along and put in a day's work anyway.

The issues raised by this story are an invitation to do some hard thinking about how the church should be involved with people whose lives have gone wrong, and the theological questions asked are: 'What happens when our prayers are not answered? What does God say about the failure of our dreams? What have we to say to the observation that in places where the church has not the courage to go, often unbelievers are carrying out the mission of God?'

6. *An Invisible Woman* is the first of a pair of stories featuring a clergy wife who has lived in her husband's shadow for so long she feels she has vanished altogether, a young man whose struggle against mental illness has scarred his life, but not his integrity, and his two friends: one a small child and the other a young man with epilepsy and Down's Syndrome. This story is about the healing and trust that this unlikely group of people find in each other's company.

The theological theme of the story is redemption, but lifted out of a churchy setting, and relocated in the setting of human friendship and acceptance. The story invites us to reflect that sometimes it is the attitudes we encounter in church that contribute to our lostness, and sometimes it is religion that the love of God has to redeem us from. Note— not faith; religion.

7. My guess is that *Sam in Love* is going to be most people's favourite story, because it is a love story and it has a happy ending. It has to be read after the story that precedes it in the book, because *Sam in Love* is the sequel. The same characters appear as in the previous story, with the addition of Eleanor, a sociology student and vicar's daughter.

The theological question of this story is the opposite of that raised in *A Dream Come True*. There we were asking: 'What happens when our prayers are not answered?', and in *Sam in Love* we are asking the opposite question: 'And what is happening when our prayers *are* answered?' What kind of God do we believe in? How does God get involved in our world?

8. The next story in the book, *A Many Splendoured Thing*, raises the controversial matter of homosexuality. Top of the list of those the church community in general rejects, despises and condemns is the gay man. In this story he is given what the church almost universally denies him: an opportunity to speak.

The theological issue addressed is the question put to Jesus by the Pharisee (ancestor of the modern churchgoer): 'Love my neighbour? And who is my neighbour?' The story is a retelling of the parable of the Good Samaritan, and though the personnel have altered, the challenge has not.

Finally, there are three short pieces, which speak for themselves. These pieces all underline the challenge of the rest of the book: to stop, to look, to listen, to think; to begin to see people as Jesus saw them—'Simon, do you see this woman?' and to discover something of his love— 'Don't be afraid. It's me'—that casts out fear.

Enjoy the stories; that's how they work, by enjoying them. They don't tell you what to think, they drop the germ of an idea inside your mind, and gradually it begins to grow until an understanding develops that did not exist before. So think of this book as a packet of seeds, and the accompanying notes as hints on planting and watering. May God the Holy Spirit give the increase!

THE STORIES

In Grosvenor Street

*'Why were you looking for me?' he replied.
'Did you not know that I must be busy with
my Father's affairs?' But they did not
understand what he meant (Luke 2:49).*

In Grosvenor Street

One hundred and eighteen minutes was how long it should have taken Dai Richards to sweep the wide arc of Duchess Crescent and back the length of Grosvenor Street, according to the national time and motion study. All I can say is, they can't have done their study on a man raised in the Welsh valleys with a 'How d'you do?' for everyone he meets and all the time in the world to say it. Normally it didn't matter—after all, he swept the streets well enough, which is what he was paid to do, and it's not everyone who's queueing up for that job, is it?

He's a reliable worker too, is Dai; been on that same stretch of road for seventeen years now, all weathers, hardly a day off sick. It was just that this morning they had to send the time and motion study fiend down to my office, and there he stood, shifting about with his clipboard, clicking his retractable ballpoint in and out till I could have stuffed it down his throat.

It was April too, which is a bad month for us. Council rates had gone up again and the phone had been rung nearly off the hook all morning, with: 'The storm drain in our road has been blocked with leaves and children's sweet wrappers for three days. We pay our rates the same

28

as anybody. When is the street sweeper coming to clear it up?'

And: 'This is Mrs Cousins from 78 Grosvenor Street, and I've got a complaint. I've been watching out of my window all morning for Mr Richards, and he hasn't been to sweep the street. It's his day, and he should have been here by now. Where is he? Do you know how much I pay in rates bills now? It's just not good enough!'

Then I had a call from his wife, asking me where Dai was because he hadn't been in for his tea-break, and that wasn't like him—Dai always arranged his round to be near his little cottage in St James' Square in time to pop in for his elevenses.

It occurred to me that perhaps he'd forgotten to plug his dust-cart in to the battery charger the night before, in which case he could be marooned, at this moment, four miles away in the middle of Grosvenor Street, which was very heavy for traffic on a midweek morning.

So, glad of any excuse to get away from the bureaucrat who was blocking up my office, I got in the car and went to look for him. He's easy enough to spot: a big, bald man in his bright red council overalls, towing a bright yellow dust-cart. I didn't like having to go searching him out, ordinarily, because I hardly ever found him doing what he should be doing. Usually he'd be in someone else's house having a quiet cup of tea, or standing with his head under the bonnet of a car at Pete's garage, helping the mechanics out with electrical faults, which were his speciality. It was a rare day when I would come upon him sweeping industriously the length of the street; but he got it done all right, given time, so who was I to complain?

Maybe this morning was different, though. I pondered it as I drove slowly down the hill towards Grosvenor Street. I didn't like the sound of him not calling in to his missus for a mid-morning cuppa. He's a real family man is Dai

Richards—proud of his kids, and loves his wife. His son had a birthday last week. Thirty-three years old he is now, Ceri Richards, and a school teacher seventy miles away in Birmingham. Dai brought in a photograph to show me: of Ceri with his class of kids. Proud as Punch of him, Dai was, and a little bit in awe too. 'Me, I can't read, nor even write my own name,' he said in wonder, 'but just look at my Ceri! Thirty-three, and head of his own department! Geography, he teaches. I always knew he'd go far, my Ceri. Shame he's had to move away, though. We don't see so much of him now.'

Then he added, quietly, 'Sometimes I wonder if he isn't a bit ashamed of his mum and dad. He doesn't come home these days.'

He looked at the photograph with affection and pride, and then he tucked the little picture away in his shirt pocket, next to his heart.

I had never met Ceri, but I knew Dai's daughter Myffanwy, because the whole family came to chapel every Sunday: Dai and Nerys, Myffanwy and her little lad Shane. 'Myffanwy,' Dai used to say to me, his voice lingering over the lilt of it. 'Isn't that music in your ears? Myffanwy. . . .'

It had been a grief to him when Myffanwy had had a child out of wedlock, but they stuck by her, he and Nerys, and Myffanwy and her little lad lived at home with them still, cramped somehow into the little cottage in St James' Square.

They'd been at chapel last Sunday, when the reading had been all about how Jesus had got lost in Jerusalem when he was just a lad. His distraught parents had found him in the Temple after all their frantic searching. There he sat, amazing the big-wigs with his wisdom, and when his mum ticked him off, all he would say was, 'Didn't you realise I must be in my Father's house, about my Father's business?'

It made me chuckle at the time. Must have been quite a handful, don't you think, Jesus?

Suddenly, I spotted Dai's dust-cart outside St Agnes' Church, which put an end to my ruminations. St Agnes' is a big Roman Catholic church, with a huge crucifix, almost life-size, outside it. Dai didn't really approve, being chapel, and used to mutter about graven images and idolatrous papists. But there he was, standing stock still in the street in his red overalls, holding his broom in one hand and his shovel in the other, staring at that crucifix.

Passers-by were going back and forth, walking round him, giving him a bit of a wide berth it seemed, glancing at him and hurrying by. I wondered if he'd been taken bad or something. By a stroke of luck I found a parking space there—usually it's murder trying to get in down there by the shops, but the rush had eased off a bit now it was pushing lunchtime. So I parked the car and got out, and he was still standing there.

'All right, Dai?' I called as I got out of the car, but he didn't respond. I shut the car door and walked over to him, put my hand on his shoulder, and he turned to look at me. His face was streaming with tears. I was so taken aback, I didn't know what to say. Then he gestured with his broom at the big crucifix.

'Look what they done to him!' he said thickly, his face red and contorted. I looked. It looked the same as usual. Nobody had done anything to it that I could see.

'Come on, Dai,' I said gently. 'Come back to the office. Your missus is worried about you. How long have you been standing here?'

I took his broom and his shovel out of his hands and flung them in the cart.

'Come on, Dai,' I said again. I steered him round to the passenger door of my car, and opened it for him. He got in like a man in a daze. I drove the car out into the road, left the hazard lights on while I climbed out again, towed the dust-cart into the parking space, then got back into my car again. Dai was wiping his eyes, and blowing his nose on a huge white handkerchief. He still looked a bit shaken up, but he was back on this planet.

'I'm sorry, Mr Burgess,' he said. 'I didn't mean to cause you trouble.'

'What's upset you, Dai?' I asked him, as we slowed down for the lights. 'Let's go for a little drive and you can tell me all about it, then I'll drop you off to your missus for your lunch.'

I was preparing myself for anything from a death in the family to Myffanwy pregnant again, but I never expected him to say, 'It was what the preacher said on Sunday.'

'On Sunday?' I repeated foolishly. 'The preacher? What?'

Dai sighed a deep, shaky sigh. 'About Jesus, when he was only a lad, and his mum and dad lost him.'

He paused, and looked at me. I smiled at him encouragingly, and then as the lights changed and we pulled away, he went on, 'When my Ceri was a little kid, not much more than four years old, we took him down to the park when they had the fair on, Nerys and me. Myffanwy'd not been born then; she came along the next year, in the spring. Ceri was our only child. And we lost him. We searched high and low for him, had the police out, gave it out on the tannoy. All afternoon we looked for him, till at twenty to five Nerys suddenly pointed and she said, "Oh, Dai, look!" And there was our Ceri, curled up fast asleep on the ground by the litter bin. I guess he figured his dad would have to come along and empty it sooner or later.

'It made me smile, that did, on Sunday. You know, I'd never thought of him like that, Jesus; a real little lad like my Ceri, wandering off like lads do, and giving his mum and dad a bit o' lip when they found him. Wouldn't be surprised if he got a clip round the ear for that.'

Dai smiled, a tender, gentle smile. He looked as though he was seeing something I couldn't see.

'But what. . . ?' I said. I was still puzzled. Does it make a man weep in the middle of Grosvenor Street, that Jesus was a real little lad like Ceri Richards? Dai looked at me, and the smile had gone. His eyes were full of sadness.

'He was my Ceri's age, thirty-three, when they nailed him to that cross. Grown up and gone away from his mum and dad, like my Ceri. Children bring you sorrow, Mr Burgess. My children have. I've lain awake nights worrying about our Myffanwy. And Ceri . . . you know, he didn't even send a card to Nerys on her birthday? He was everything to us, but it seems like he doesn't want to know us any more. There's no mum or dad but knows what sorrow is. But what would our Nerys do, if she had to stand and watch our Ceri hanging on a cross?

'Mr Burgess, I've been a Christian and a true believer since I was seven years old. Made my commitment in a Welsh chapel, far away from here. Forty-six years I've been a Christian and I'd go to the stake saying that Jesus is God and Lord of everything. But it was only today I saw it all of a sudden, as clear and sharp as can be, that Jesus was a man too; a young man like my Ceri. And look what we did to him, Mr Burgess. Look what we did to him.'

I left him with Nerys, still with that pain and tenderness and sadness trembling all around him. I hoped Nerys would understand, because I'm sure I didn't. We don't have that many visionaries working for the Council.

It was all a bit deep for me, and I felt almost jealous of Dai Richards, that I couldn't see what he saw, be moved as he was moved by the broken humanity of Jesus. The thought uppermost in my mind, as I drove back to the office, was that I was none too sure the time and motion man was going to understand it either.

Time to Put Things Right

. . . a shelter from the wind,
a refuge from the storm,
like streams of water in dry places,
like the shade of a great rock in a thirsty land (Isaiah 32:2).

Time to Put Things Right

The morning started out well enough, with just a fine mist of rain struggling unevenly with a watery sun. It was the sun that lost, and by midday I was soaked to the skin and trudged doggedly under a relentless deluge of stinging rain. My hair was plastered uncomfortably to my forehead and cheekbones, and cold rivulets of rain trickled depressingly down my scalp and neck, losing themselves in my sodden clothes.

Rain dripped from the end of my nose. Rain trickled down my face and into my mouth. My pack dragged on my shoulders in an unremitting, sullen ache, and my boots squelched, heavy with water.

My progress was slowed by my wet clothes. The sodden, cold, heavy fabric of my trousers stuck dismally to my calves and thighs. The path had turned to sloppy mud which sucked and gurgled round my feet as I toiled up the hill. I could hardly see five yards ahead of me in the grey, driving downpour.

I had long since lost my way, and I blundered along path after path amid the endless dreary tracts of conifers, every one the same and not a soul in sight. A nauseating lump of equal parts self-pity and hunger grew until it sat like a stone in the pit of my stomach. In the end I was walking because it was better than standing still; walking because there was nowhere to sit down; walking because it offered a pretended alternative to the misery and childish humiliation of being lost and upset and cold.

The little flint house behind its low pale of wicket fencing seemed like a gift of the angels as I came through the black, dripping trees into the clearing. I hesitated for no longer than the briefest of seconds before I plunged up the path and, picking up the stout iron knocker, belted it good and hard on the door.

It was opened after a moment or two by a man some forty years my senior—for he must have been seventy easily.

'I've lost my way. . . .'

What was intended as a sort of polite and humorous beginning blurted out instead as a distressed entreaty. Without a word he stood back from the doorway, gesturing me in to the warm refuge of his snug little house. My boots, weighted with water, caught on the threshold and I half-stepped, half-stumbled inside.

The door opened directly into the front room of the house, and when he shut it behind me I felt more than a little awkward as I stood dripping on his living room floor. It's amazing how far a little water can go—that's one of life's first lessons, isn't it? I couldn't help thinking how Daphne would have reacted, and waited dumbly, half-expecting the familiar torrent of shrewish bitterness. Instead came the man's quiet Scots voice: 'I cannot offer you dry things to wear, for you'd make two of me, young man. But you're welcome to a blanket and my fireside while we get the worst of the wet out of those clothes.'

He spoke with the same practical warmth with which he had welcomed me into his house a few moments before. I suppose you could call him kind, but he had none of the effusiveness I normally associate with kindness. He did not even smile. I felt more like his son than his guest. It was like coming home; and I felt no embarrassment any more as I peeled off my dripping clothes, handing them to him one by one until I stood like a white ghost, steaming before his fire.

He took the drenching bundle through to the adjoining kitchen, where I heard the splatter of them being dumped into the sink. Then I heard the stairs and the floorboards overhead creaking under his feet. A moment later he returned, carrying a coarse towel and a blue woollen blanket.

'Make yourself comfortable,' he said as he tossed them into my arms before disappearing once more into the kitchen. I could hear him rinsing my clothes, wringing them out, the slap of them being shaken out and the rattle of the airer as he lowered it, hung the clothes, and ran it up to the ceiling again.

I rubbed myself down and, opening my wet pack over by the door, I retrieved some damp jeans and underpants and a damper shirt, and spread them to dry on the fender. Then, gratefully, I wrapped myself in his blanket and sank in a weary ecstasy of relief into the shabby fireside arm-chair, stretching my sore feet in front of me on the rug and closing my eyes with a deep sigh of contentment.

It might have been the clatter of crockery that awoke me, for when I opened my eyes again, the first thing they fell upon was a steaming mug of hot tea and a solid wedge of fruit cake, and cheese to go with it, waiting beside me on a kitchen chair.

It was hardly good manners I suppose, but my mouth watered at the sight of it, and I just couldn't wait. I fell on it like a wolf, eating it in great hungry bites, drinking the tea in scalding gulps, dropping crumbs everywhere. Some-where in the edge of my mind I could hear Daphne, see her even, the stillness of her disapproval, the icy, with-ering voice—'Can't you eat quietly? Can't you eat slowly?

You look like an animal attacking that food. You look disgusting. You look. . . .'

I looked up as I heard his chuckle in the kitchen doorway.

'I was coming to ask you if you take sugar in your tea. I'm a bit late, I see. My word! And there's a hole to fill yet, I should think!'

I began to mumble apologies, ashamed of my greediness, but he cut me short: 'There's no offence in hunger, my friend. Those clothes you've hung by the fire will be dry now, if you want to dress yourself while I find you something a bit more substantial to eat.'

'Oh no, really . . .' I began to protest, anxious about the imposition I was making, insisting I should be on my way.

But even as I spoke, I took in that the lowering gloom of the afternoon was descending into the darkness of evening, and the rain was still deluging its way towards night.

'Supper, and a bed for the night,' said my host firmly. 'You're all the same, you young men nowadays; you can't read a map, nor use a compass, nor even walk in a straight line. How do you think you'd fare on a wet night with no stars, now? Supper, young man, and bed.'

He spoke with unsmiling severity, but there was a twinkle in his eye as he came and took my empty plate and mug, and disappeared with them into the kitchen.

The clothes I had draped on the fender were warm and dry now, and good to put on. As I dressed myself, I caught the appetising odour of hot, savoury food drifting from the kitchen. When I followed through the door and saw the table spread with bread (a good, big, new, brown loaf) and butter and cheddar cheese and pickles and thick, meaty soup and the rest of the fruit cake, a feeling of such contentment welled up in me as I had almost forgotten was possible.

He asked me, as we ate, where I was bound, and I admitted ruefully that I was an inexperienced walker; that I'd lost my way in the maze of paths through the pine forests. I confessed with a smile that I'd been blundering about, completely lost and cursing the whole expedition when I came upon his cottage. As for my destination . . . well . . . I wasn't so much walking to as away from. I tried to make a joke of it, without much success, then turned the conversation onto another track, asking him if he thought the weather would lift by morning. He grimaced, pessimistically: 'It'll let up maybe one hour or two, but . . . well, once it rains, it rains, in these parts. No, it's here to stay, lad; I'm sorry.'

After we had eaten, and washed up the meal things, he made coffee, which we took by the fire; I in his armchair, and he on a low stool. I was able to get a really good look at him as he sat before me, bending now and then to put another stick on the fire, but otherwise gazing peacefully into its slowly-drawing glow.

Peaceful was the word for him. With his hard, sinewy frame and his weathered, seamed face, he looked like the trees he lived among. His hair was grizzled and sparse, his eyebrows bushy over brown eyes that twinkled amid a network of lines and wrinkles. His nose jutted over a mouth set firm in a line that was almost grim, but for the softening touch of humour there. The set of his jaw had an uncompromising look to it; it reminded me of the scarred old rocks that lay about on the open hills.

The whole of the man was solid and strong and tough, and the peace that breathed out of him was like it too. I've never known anything like it anywhere. It was tangible, that peace. You could rest your back on it, the way you can lean on an oak tree, and feel the rough, supporting warmth of it. You could get your teeth into it like you could into his thick slices of bread and butter, and feel its richness nourishing your hungry soul. A solid, unshakeable peace that filled the room with a quality of eternity, from the low rafters to the oil-cloth on the floor.

The other extraordinary thing about this extraordinary

man was the gentleness of his hands. Gently they had taken the bread—almost lovingly—and broken it. Gently his hands held the cup as he gave me my drink—you could say reverently, even. His hands were gentle as he handled the crockery when we washed up the meal things together. Let me make myself clear. I don't mean there was anything uncertain about his grasp or timorous in his movements. His hands were muscular, with the raised veins and strong fingers of a workman. Now, as he sat by the hearth and picked up the small logs and placed them in the fire, the movements of his hands were firm, precise, but—gentle.

He'd let my eyes devour him long enough, I suppose, for he turned now to look at me.

'It's a queer thing, the way men come walking over these hills, away from their troubles. Over the hills and far away, they think. But, far away . . . far away is like a mirage that shimmers always on the horizon, and they find their troubles walk with them, as fast attached as their own shadows.'

He asked no question, and I appreciated that, but it was an invitation. He studied me a moment longer, then his gaze wandered again to the fire. He picked up the poker, and prodded the logs thoughtfully. As I watched the little shower of sparks and the fall of ash, I felt all the familiar bitterness rise up in me like gall, and I was stirred by a returning wave of the restless anger that had fired me at the beginning of the day. Well, I would tell him.

My mouth twisted with the sour memory of old injustices. A father who had made a favourite of my brother and given him all the help he needed, left me floundering. If I'd had the same hand-up as Ray, I wouldn't be in the mess I was in now. A wife who cheated on me—bitch! A boss at work who passed me over and passed me over. Struggle and more struggle and betrayal and unfairness.

I opened my mouth to speak, and he turned and looked at me. His brown eyes looked into mine, and mine glared back out of the torture of resentment and frustration that had become my accustomed shackles. As I started to tell my story, all the peace of the man, tangible peace, held me, took firm hold of me. The words that came out were not the story I had opened my mouth to tell. It was more like a confession. I told him of my shame and bitter failure; of my cowardice and inadequacy, my disappointment and fear. I told him about the drinking and the debts that had made chaos of my marriage; and after a long pause full of shame, I found it in me to tell him how I had lied and lied and lied.

As I told it out, a strange thing happened. The peace that was coming from him, that filled the room and held me fast, began to probe into my soul, peeling away layer after layer of my defences as I told the sorry story, stripping them away like wet clothes, until I had nothing. And then, both of us were left looking at the rotten wound where my heart should have been: a sore, sickening, hurting, lonely place. He said nothing, and I had no more to say. I sat swallowing back tears, faced it at last: despair's spectre.

His hands were still now, resting on his knees, veined and calloused, work-hard hands. But somehow—how can I tell it?—it was as though all the gentleness in them gathered itself, became hands on its own, and touched that raw, hurting place that was all that was left of me; and I nearly cried out under the pain of that gentleness. I thought I couldn't stand it as the gentleness that had made itself into hands cleaned and dressed and dealt with the sore and broken thing I had become. I gasped with it, looked down at my bare feet, stared at the pattern on the oil-cloth, shook.

'Sleep on it, lad,' came the slow Scottish voice, and I looked up, dazed.

'There's a bed for you upstairs. Sleep on it. There's time to put things right.'

I was up with the dawn the next morning, but he was before me, lighting the fire, making porridge. I took mine with sugar, and he took his with salt.

'I've aired your things,' he said, as we sat and ate together. 'They're dry enough, and your boots are no wetter than they would be anyway after half an hour's walking in this mud.'

He asked me where I was headed for, so as to redirect me onto my way. I hesitated.

'I've lost a day. The clouds are heavy again. I think. . . .' It hung in the balance for a moment, but really I'd made up my mind. And I knew when I spoke the words that the healing was real, held good.

'I think I'll go home,' I said.

Release

Treat others as you would like them to treat you.
If you love those who love you, what thanks can
you expect? Even sinners love those who love them.
And if you do good to those who do good to you,
what thanks can you expect? For even sinners do that
much. And if you lend to those from whom you hope
to receive, what thanks can you expect? Even sinners
lend to sinners to get back the same amount (Luke 6: 31–34).

Release

I thought it might have been a mistake as soon as I'd asked him to come. I wasn't so much worried about him saying 'no', as terrified that he might say 'yes'. And, of course, he did.

I didn't feel sure, not at all sure, that our house group was ready for my brother Jim. But I couldn't have asked him to sit in the kitchen while everyone else talked and laughed in the living room, could I?

Of course, it was unfortunate that my turn had come round to have the house group that very week. There again, I could have put him off until the following week, but . . . oh, if you'd seen the look in his eyes when he realised that was what I was hinting at. All the bravado and the cheeky grin went shaky all of a sudden, and he looked down suddenly, his hands twisting tight together on the table.

'They won't release me without an address to go to,' he said, and I couldn't stand the disappointment and the plea in his voice. Mum and Dad didn't want anything to do with him, you see; not any more. They'd paid to put him through public school and paid for his university degree course, and considered this a very poor return for their money. I suppose it was, but I didn't feel like they did. I'd visited him all along. It was just a bit awkward with it being house group on Wednesday, because I could see he'd have to be invited and . . . oh dear . . . I could just imagine it.

Anyway, I said he could come to me. He had nowhere else, after all. His landlady didn't want him back—she'd made that plain.

'Thanks, Sue,' he said, very serious, a bit strained, not like himself at all.

I was a bit short with him Wednesday teatime, I must admit, as he sat on my kitchen table drinking lager and smoking one of his wretched roll-ups, watching me cook his tea.

'You'll put that beer can in the outside bin when you've finished with it, won't you?' I said, a bit snappy and cross.

'Whatever for? It's raining,' he replied, puzzled.

'Sometimes Maggie helps me to make the coffee, and I don't want her to see a beer can in my bin. It's bad enough having the stink of cigarette smoke all through the flat.'

I was getting irritable, and Jim was staring at me in amazement.

'Why didn't you say? I'll just smoke in the bedroom if you like. I—'

'Oh, never mind! I don't care if you smoke, it's just today. The people from church won't approve. None of them smoke or drink, and it's—oh, you don't understand, Jim.'

He didn't. He stubbed out the cigarette without a word, drained off the remains of his can of beer, and went outside to the dustbin with the empty can and the saucer he had used as an ashtray. When he came back in, he wiped his feet very deliberately on the mat, went to the sink and washed the ashtray, very carefully, in silence.

I felt upset and annoyed, and I burned my hand with a splash of hot fat as I turned the egg over in the frying pan.

'Oh, sh—' I started to say, and amended it to, 'Oh, sugar!'

That was his fault too. His bad ways were catching. The ladies from church had prayed with me for weeks about my swearing, and they'd been so pleased for me when I'd conquered it at last. I mustn't slip back into it again. I turned round and looked at Jim, drying his saucer on a tea-towel, bitterly meticulous.

'Your tea's ready,' I said.

His eyes looked dark and strange as he looked back at me, half-defiant, half-vulnerable. It had changed him, there was no doubt about that.

He sat down at the table, fiddling with his knife and fork while I put his food on a plate.

'Would you rather I went out tonight, Sue?'

Yes! I wanted to shout at him. Yes! Yes! But the way he asked it hurt me, because I could feel it hurting him. So instead I said, 'Oh, Jim, of course not. Come on, eat your tea.'

I sat down opposite him and watched him pushing the food round his plate. I could do without this, really.

'I'm not such a bad lad, Susie. I was only in for a bit of puff.'

He said it very quietly, and he didn't look up.

'Your egg's getting cold,' I replied. I felt a bit ashamed. If it had been Bob, or Maggie, or Helen from house group sitting in front of me, as unsure and as vulnerable as he was, I'd have jumped to my feet and put my arms round them, but I felt awkward with Jim. We never were all that demonstrative in our family.

He put a forkful of food in his mouth, and I got up to make a pot of tea.

'Why aren't you eating?' he said.

'I don't know,' I hedged. 'I can't really fancy anything tonight.'

Well, what else could I have said? I could hardly turn round and tell him I was too nervous at the thought of the people from church meeting my brother; too worried about what he'd put his foot in it and say, could I? I might as well have said it straight out, though. He's not stupid, whatever else he is. He finished his tea in silence.

Keith and Helen arrived first, and Allen and Valerie followed them in. They were laughing over a story Allen had been telling them in the car, and it was such a relief to have their cheerful faces lift the tension that filled the flat. They hugged me and took off their coats as they came into the living room.

'Oh gosh, you poor thing!' exclaimed Valerie. 'What a smell of cigarettes! Have you been counselling someone?'

I laughed and got out to the kitchen as quickly as I could, saying something about making coffee. Jim was sitting on the table, with his feet on one of the chairs, his shoulders hunched. He'd just rolled a cigarette, and he was rolling it back and forth in his fingers, unlit, his head bent. He looked up at me suddenly, his eyes bright, smiling cynically.

'Have a simply super evening, sister,' he said sarcastically. 'I'm just off to the pub to get totally immersed.'

'Why do you have to be so *difficult*?' I hissed at him through clenched teeth.

'I don't know,' he said, laying his hand on his heart and looking at me with wicked mockery. 'Perhaps you'd better lift me up to the Lord in prayer.'

Then he pocketed his cigarette papers and tobacco, and went, taking with him the last of my housekeeping money which I'd lent him on a misguided impulse of kindness at lunchtime.

I heard him in the hall saying, 'Oh, *do* excuse me,' as he passed Bob and Mike and Maggie on their way in, then he slammed the door behind him. In that moment, my brother or not, I hated him.

I pinned a smile onto my face as I took the tray of coffee into the living room, bracing myself for the inevitable question.

'Susie, whoever was that?' Maggie asked as she took off her anorak.

'My brother,' I said, with careful nonchalance. 'He came out of prison on Monday.'

The split second of silence that followed confirmed all my anxieties.

'Oh, I'm sorry, Sue, I didn't realise . . .' Maggie gasped, her cheeks pink. I busied myself handing round the coffee.

'I didn't know you had a brother, Sue,' said Mike. 'What's his name?'

I could have hugged Mike. It had been a long time since Jim's name meant more to someone than his prison sentence did. Most people said, 'What's he done?'

'Jim,' I answered. 'My little brother Jim.'

The others applied themselves earnestly to their coffee, but Mike asked, 'Didn't he want to join us?'

I wasn't sure how to answer him. I wasn't sure what the answer was. I hadn't been able to make myself invite him.

'He's a bit touchy about it all,' I said. That was true, at any rate.

'How long is he staying?' asked Helen, casually. Too casually. But of course, her children were supposed to be coming for the morning tomorrow, while she went to the hairdresser.

'He'll be here tomorrow, if that's what you mean,' I said defensively. She looked at me, sorry, pleading.

'I'm sorry, Sue, but I couldn't. . . . Emma and Matthew are so young still. I'm sorry. Another time.'

'It's all right,' I said quickly. 'I do understand. Actually, I think I'd feel the same myself. Can we change the subject now? Shall we make a start?'

The singing didn't go too well, I must admit, so we moved on to the Bible study. We were studying the symbolism of the book of Daniel. I couldn't seem to concentrate on it somehow, and most of it just flowed over my head that evening. Mike kept looking at me as though he wanted to say something, but I was careful not to catch his eye.

Keith's turn had come to lead that evening, and after we'd waded through four chapters, he said we'd leave the rest for next time because it seemed a bit heavy going. He suggested that we should move into a time of prayer.

We all bent our heads, and Keith had started to say, 'We just really praise you, Lord, that we can meet together like this, Lord; that in this country we're free to—' when the front door opened with a crash that made me jump half out of my skin. We heard it slam shut, and Jim lurched in with a bottle of cider in one hand and a cigarette in the other.

Looking up at him, my heart sank. His eyes blurred in a dull fog of dope and alcohol. I was appalled to imagine whatever cocktail of poisons he had in his bloodstream. He could see us, but I think that was the best you could say. I'd seen the last of my housekeeping money, that much was evident. He had the total, startled, silent attention of everyone.

He grinned at us, and leaned on the wall. He took a swig of his cider, tipping some down the front of his shirt. 'Oh, shit,' he said. I suppose I should have been glad it was nothing worse.

'Hello, Jim,' said Mike.

'I don't think we've been introduced,' Jim replied loftily. 'Or has my reputation gone before me?' He looked at me, and I felt embarrassed by the challenge in his eyes. He didn't trust me to defend him, then. And why should he? No one else had stuck by him.

None of us spoke. Nobody knew what to say. Jim leaned forward slightly and focused on us with a bit of an effort. I felt my stomach tying itself into knots. I could see he was absolutely out of his brain. I dreaded to think what we had coming.

'Grey and frozen, frozen and grey we dance round each other.' Jim started to speak, his voice bitter and hard. 'The indecent and silent pavanne of wraiths who must gain what sensuality they can get from peeping through bedroom windows, from sucking the blood of somebody else's life.'

He paused and looked at us, contemptuous, aggressive.

'Why can't we say what we mean? Why do we shrivel at one another's touch? Why do we paint our faces and comb our hair? To make paper dragons of ourselves? Insubstantial images, weaving in and out of the frigid carnival.'

He had a bit of a struggle with the word 'insubstantial', but the rest came out clear enough. I wished the floor would swallow me up. I had worried, goodness knows, about the part of my life that was Jim coming into contact with the part of my life that was house group, but even my worst imaginings hadn't been as bad as this. And he hadn't finished yet. He took another gulp of cider and wiped the back of his mouth with his hand. Then he carried on.

'There was a man once, and he *knew* how to party. Six, but *six* bloody great thirty gallon jars of wine; velvet on your lips, delight of fiery sweet potency sliding round your mouth. . . .'

Valerie averted her eyes and blushed, and Helen and Maggie both simultaneously crossed their legs. I felt an insane desire to giggle rising up inside me. He hadn't finished yet.

'He made it out of water! Hic—pardon me—out of water! Water mixed with the power of God! Oh, mix that power with our water! Give us your fiery, sweet, full-bodied potency, power of God!'

He paused, and looked round the room. 'Oh, Lord,' I prayed silently, 'stop him. Please stop him. Oh, please.'

'It's not that we don't need something more than all this,' Jim went on. The aggression had gone from his voice now; it sounded passionate still, but also sad. 'We come looking, circling round each other, with our ghostly smiles,

our hollow social laughter, our vapid gestures. Oh,
God. . . .'

His mouth twisted suddenly and his face crumpled. For
one awful moment I thought he was really going to make a
fool of himself and cry, but then he took another pull at his
cider and carried on. You could have heard a pin drop. He
closed his eyes.

'. . . oh, God. Can you save us, even from whistling in
the dark? Can you rescue us from the sad motley of our
songs and smiles, our ragged courage and the decking out
of our broken hearts?

'This one, whose hand trembles, whose face is bent to
hide his tears, concentrating on the flimsy shelter of lighting a cigarette . . . or this one, who declaims from the
pulpit, urgent and intent, with an answer for all the
world's aches and no salve for his own . . . or this one,
immaculately dressed in a careful smile and high-heeled
shoes, slimmed to perfection, coloured in and cut out and
propped up on show. . . .'

His voice had dropped to a whisper, but there was no
stopping him.

'Have you anything to save us from this? Is there any
means by which we can step down from our pretence, and
overcoming our revulsion and our fear, win through to
tenderness?'

I opened my mouth to speak, but Mike reached out
quickly and laid a hand on my arm. He frowned at me
and shook his head. Nobody else moved. Jim stood there,
his eyes closed, ash dropping from his cigarette onto my
carpet. Drunk he might be, but he meant what he was
saying all right, and he went on still in the same yearning
whisper: 'I know that I have done now with the masquer-
ade, and stand awkward and lonely, naked and ashamed. I
have stretched out a timid hand, and I am waiting. A slap
in the face? Cold indifference? Embarrassment? I dare not
hope for what I yearn for: an honest hand grasping mine,

eyes meeting eyes, acceptance, integrity. . . . Should I hope for it? You, naked and lonely, they crucified. If I too should be broken on that cross, and find in such distress your fellowship, I would have a hundred times satisfaction for the anguish of my heart's hunger. . . .'

I looked round the room. Mike was leaning forward in his chair, his eyes fixed on Jim's face as if there was no one else in all the world. Helen's lips were pursed, and her foot was switching from side to side in a small, contained, irritated motion. Keith's mouth hung slightly ajar. Valerie and Allen and Maggie and Bob just sat frozen in their seats. Jim closed his eyes tighter, and a spasm of pain went over his face. He had gone very pale.

Then, without warning, he was copiously sick all over the carpet. I couldn't believe it. I just couldn't believe it. I sat looking at the pointed toe of Helen's black, patent leather, high-heeled shoe, dappled with vomit, and I couldn't believe it. This couldn't be happening to me.

'Keith,' Helen said, in a quiet, flat voice, and he closed his mouth and jumped to attention. She got up without another word, and picked her way across the room.

'I'll get your coats,' I said miserably, but, 'No, no. No, no,' Keith stopped me. 'That's quite all right. We'll see ourselves out. No, no, don't get up for us. You've got enough on your hands, I think.' And he laughed in a high, nervous sort of way. Gathering up their coats, he followed Helen out to the car.

'D'you think they've forgotten they're giving us a lift?' Allen asked Valerie. 'I'd better go and see.' And he went out after Keith and Helen, and came back a moment later, saying, 'Come on!' to Valerie. She grabbed their Bibles and anoraks, and gave my shoulder a sympathetic little squeeze on her way out. 'It'll be all right,' she said.

I just sat there. I couldn't believe it.

Bob and Maggie looked at each other, then they got up to go too.

'I'm sorry, Sue,' said Bob, lamely. 'It seems a bit early to be going, but Jo's baby-sitting, and she's got exams coming up, and . . . well, you know. Are you coming, Mike?'

Mike shook his head. 'I'll make my own way home,' he said. Jim flopped down into the armchair Bob had just vacated. Mike took the cider bottle from his hand, and the cigarette, which had gone out on its own and hung forlornly between Jim's fingers. He was still as white as a sheet, and he sat looking at the vomit on the carpet.

'Oh, shit. I'm sorry, Susie,' he said.

'It's all right,' I replied wearily. What else could I say?

It was Mike who helped me get Jim to bed when he passed out five minutes later, and Mike who helped me clear up the mess. You know, I like Mike. It had gone midnight before I saw him out. He gave me a hug as he left.

'He's quite something, your brother,' he said with a grin. 'I'd like to meet him again. That's the first prayer I've heard in a long time that I could say "Amen" to. You didn't say he was a Christian.'

I shook my head. 'As far as I know, he's not. At least not when he's sober. Anyway, thanks for all your help, Mike.'

I shut the door behind him, and leaned my back against it with a sigh.

So now they knew. I wondered what they'd think of me, but I wasn't anxious any more. It was too late now for pretending, and somehow that was a tremendous relief. Anyway, Mike wanted to come back and meet Jim again, and you know—I like Mike.

I put the light out in the hall, and walked through to the bedroom. Jim lay spark out on the mattress on the floor, exactly as we'd left him.

I curled up on my bed with my 'Day by Day' notes, to do my Bible reading and quiet time. Blow me if the reading for the day wasn't the story of the wedding at Cana, from the second chapter of John's Gospel. I couldn't help it, I just lay on my bed and laughed.

Jim had blown my house group to bits, and my flat stank of cider and vomit and disinfectant and cigarettes and fried food. But in an odd, irrelevant way, all I could think of was that I didn't have to have Helen's children in the morning. And it was such a relief.

The Perfect Host

Do this in remembrance of me (Luke 22:19, NIV).

The Perfect Host

It was the night Kathy ditched me that I heard about Jesus. We kept our phone in the kitchen, and our mum was doing the ironing there when it rang.

'Trevor!'

She had to shout four times up the stairs. I was blasting my ears with the heaviest, meanest rock of all my tapes, loud enough to shrivel my brain and numb the disappointment that ached inside because Kathy hadn't phoned.

'Trevor!'

In a pause between two tracks I heard her yell, and I stopped the tape.

'Trevor! It's Kath on the phone for you!'

I almost fell down the stairs, and floated into the kitchen. The aching had hatched out into butterflies and they were tickling my insides. I grabbed the phone.

'Kath?'

She said what she had to say, and Mum put her iron down and stood watching me while I listened to it. I didn't ask Kathy her reasons—what good would that have done? Who cares about reasons why when the stars are lying broken on the ground at your feet and the birds have forgotten how to sing and your heart feels like it might be bleeding?

I just said, 'OK,' and she said goodbye, and for a moment it felt as though the world had stopped. Not goodbye. Oh, not goodbye. 'Kath, wait a minute—' but I heard the click as she put the phone down. It was over. I couldn't quite believe it. I stood looking stupidly at the receiver in my hand; didn't want to put it down. That would make it final, wouldn't it, hanging up the phone and walking away?

'Oh, Trevor—' Mum started to say, and then I put the phone down fast enough.

'Not now, Mum,' I said, and I was out of the door and out of the house before she had time to get round the ironing board.

It was a wet, black, October night, and I stood shivering on the cracked cement of our path, letting the rain soak my shirt and the wind lash me. Where do you go when the world has ended?

I started walking, aimlessly. Every fibre of me was quivering and taut and hurting. The hopeless misery built up and up until I felt I couldn't bear it; thought it would break me apart. But instead of that I put my fist through someone's garage door in Beecham Road, and then ran like the wind when I heard the house door opening. I didn't stop running till I got down to the beach, and then I stood on the shore and looked at the boiling, crashing surf, and wondered if I had the courage . . . wondered what it felt like when your lungs were bursting for air and your head was going under and you had to take a breath, but instead of air you breathed cold, gritty seawater . . . and I didn't have the courage.

So I picked up stones, big ones, from the shingle beach, and flung them as far as I could into the thundering sea. But after a while I stopped that and just stood shivering in my shirt in the rain and the wind and the spray. What

now? Where *do* you go when the world has ended? I
clenched my fists and flung back my head, and with everything that was in me I screamed out the most obscene word
I knew at the indifferent sky.

Oh, Kathy.

I walked along the prom, shivering, and wished I'd some
money in my pocket to buy a bottle of general anaesthetic
at the pub. I had a bit of change, but when I stopped under
a streetlamp to look, I hadn't even enough for a glass of
lemonade and shelter from the rain. My knuckles were cut
and aching from their argument with the garage door;
stinging with seaspray. I was freezing. All my anger was
spent. I just felt miserable, bruised, empty, cold. Really
cold.

Oh, Kathy.

But I didn't want to go home, so I kept walking, away
from the sea, into the seedy jumble of houses at this end of
the town. In the centre, among the lights of the cinema and
the cafés, there would be people about, but here the streets
were almost deserted. An old man, stopping for his dog to
pee against the wall; a girl clutching her coat tight around
her, her head bent against the rain, running home. The
clack of her high-heeled shoes rang from the next street
long after she turned the corner out of sight.

The houses here looked like my own home, built in
terraces, steps up to the front doors, steps down to the
dark basement flats below. They were all divided into
flats—too many families, not enough money. Rotting
window-frames were held together with angle-irons and
the ugly grey rendering was cracked on the damp walls,
or simply falling off. At the corner of the street a closed-
down fish and chip shop terminated the row, its white-
washed windows plastered with torn advertisement bills.
Across the road from that the shabby red brick Gospel
Hall stood alone in its car park overgrown with weeds
and halfheartedly fenced with wire netting that lurched

round three-quarters of it then disintegrated into its own tangles among the dead stalks of summer ragwort and nettles. It was a fence for keeping nobody out and nobody in; a fence for collecting the litter that drifted across the car park. In the far corner an abandoned car decomposed quietly under a tarpaulin, with the same look of hopeless collapse about it as the overcooked chickens our mum exhumed from the oven every Sunday lunchtime.

Tonight, one or two other cars stood in the yard, and the puddled ruts reflected light from the windows of the hall. I could hear music playing inside. I walked round to the front of it, where a sign attached to the wall read: '*Church of England Evangelistic Mission*'. The paint was peeling off, but I could just make out the words underneath—'You are not your own. You were bought at a price.' Wouldn't surprise me. We were behind with the HP on the living room furniture, two months in arrears with the rent, and our mum had made us all hide in the kitchen with the door shut when the milkman came. You are not your own. You were bought at a price. Yes.

The door stood ajar. Sometimes you could get a cup of coffee there for only a few pence. I went in. Warmth!

The place was full of chairs, but there were only about ten people there. They were all singing songs from song-books, led by two lads about my age playing guitars at the front. A girl stood just inside the door holding a pile of songbooks. The wind and the rain had draggled her hair, and the parka she wore was more damp than dry. She held out a songbook to me and smiled, such a big, happy smile I almost smiled back. I hadn't planned to spend the evening singing, but I took the book—well, why not? No coffee, but at least it was warm.

I went and sat down in one of the empty rows of chairs near the back.

After a while, a few more people came in. A couple of blokes in motorbike leathers blundered into my row, and sat making comments and laughing, nudging each other and tipping their chairs back. They didn't take any notice of me though.

Then the singing stopped, and a young man got up to speak; thin, nervous sort of bloke with glasses. The lads in my row turned round the chairs in front of them so they could put their feet up. They sat back in their places with their arms folded, still making loud remarks to each other and sniggering a bit.

I moved to the end of the row by the radiator. It was blowing a gale outside and the rain spattered angrily against the black squares of window pane.

Oh, Kathy.

The skinny young bloke at the front was talking about Jesus, asking if we ever thought about how much Jesus loved us. Can't say I ever had, really. Why should I? But as I listened, it got hold of me, what he was saying about how Jesus died. As he described it, I could see it in my mind. See the man heaving and struggling to carry his cross, his back raw with the flogging they gave him, his knees buckling under him, all the people watching him, lining the roadside to see him stumble and fall, crash onto his knees on the rough flags of the street, his eyes blinded with sweat, his body trembling with exhaustion.

I could see the hard, brawny hand of the soldier, finger and thumb positioning the nail just right, the other hand a fist around the hammer, raised to thud home the first blow. I could see the pale, veined inner side of the wrist waiting exposed on the wood of the cross, with the point of the nail positioned there by the soldier's finger and thumb, and the sickening moment when the hammer crashed down and the man on the cross cried out, his body arching in a convulsion of pain, his face screwed up in agony, his lips snarling back from his teeth, his flayed back scraping against the wood of the cross, his hand convulsed into a claw.

Then, slumping again, trembling, his other hand extended for the nail, every fibre of him quivering and taut and hurting, the pain and the fear building up and up until he thought he couldn't bear it, felt as though it must break him apart. And it did. It did. Three hours he hung there struggling instinctively against the suffocation of his body's hanging from the nails that held him, then he flung back his head and with everything that was in him he cried out, 'My God, my God, why have you forsaken me?' to the indifferent sky. And then it was finished.

The skinny guy was still talking. About how Jesus wondered, the night before when he prayed out in the darkness of the garden, if he had the courage to go through with it. He'd seen men crucified, knew what the score was, wondered if he could face it, wondered what it felt like when your lungs were bursting for air, but you no longer had the strength to struggle from the nails in your feet to the nails in your hands, shifting the agony of the weight back and forth. And he did have the courage. He loved us enough for that. It made him sweat with fear to think about it. You bet it did. It . . . it made him cry, the bloke said. But he did it. He loved us enough. I wasn't sure what it all had to do with loving us, though.

Then suddenly the thin man had stopped his preach and was saying, 'Come forward if you want to give your heart to Jesus.' He said they would sing a hymn and we could 'respond', as he put it. I didn't know about responding, and as for giving my heart to Jesus, well . . . my heart was broken, definitely out of order just now. Not much use to anyone.

They started to sing, and nobody moved. The skinny preacher had his hands pressed together and his eyes tight shut. His lips were moving in a prayer, for us infidels I guess. We sang two more verses, and nobody moved.

Then a great wave of anger and sadness washed through me, leaving its spray on my face, blinding me, for that man's death. I thought about him sweating with fear, crashing to his knees in the street, with all that nightmare ahead of him. . . . And I didn't want to be part of it—what they did to him, I mean. It sounds daft, I suppose, but I wanted to make it up to him, somehow. I wanted to comfort him. Oh, Jesus, it must have hurt.

I clutched hold of my songbook a minute longer, then I put it down and shoved past the two bikers in my row, who were still sitting with their feet up, grinning, but a bit quieter now.

I stumbled up to the front and stood there, and my knees were shaking and my hands sweating. I could feel the people's eyes on my back. I didn't know why I was standing there, but I found myself whispering over and over again, 'I'm sorry. I'm sorry. I'm sorry.'

And . . . well I wasn't going to say it, but I might as well say it: I was crying. Crying for me and Kathy, crying for Jesus, crying for all the sorrow that was breaking and crashing like the surf inside me.

The Gospel Hall people gave me a book; a little blue book with a cross on the front, called *The Gospel of Luke*. They gave me this book, and they told me to read it, and they gave me a piece of paper where they'd written the address of a house in Flanders Road. They said I could go round there next Thursday, to what they called a 'nurture group'. It meant walking three miles across to the other side of town, but then I didn't have anything else to do with my evenings now, did I? Besides, it sounded kind of nice, a nurture group. I didn't know what it was, but I felt badly in need of a bit of nurturing, so I said I'd go.

It was late by the time I got home. Mum had given me up and gone to bed. I made myself a mug of tea. I took it up to my room, and sat thinking. Outside the wind had dropped. Everything quiet now, and dark, except for the yellow light of the streetlamps shining in at the window.

I felt different. The inside of me was still grieving and

broken up because of Kathy. I was dead tired. But it felt as though . . . as though someone sat there with me.

When my dad left, I was just eight; he left on the day after my birthday. He took just about everything that was his, and Mum went round the house after him, collecting everything he'd forgotten. She packed it into carrier bags, and put them in the passage by the front door. But he'd left his winter overcoat hanging in the broom cupboard. They both forgot about that, but I hadn't.

I crept downstairs, the night he left. I got inside the broom cupboard, where it was stuffy and warm, and I pulled the overcoat off its hanger and held it in my arms, with my face pressed into it. I rubbed my cheek against the rough fabric, breathing in the smell of him: clan tobacco and beer and sweat and manhood. It was almost like having him there with me. Almost, but not quite. Just enough to comfort me, and just enough to break my heart.

In the morning, Mum found me there asleep. She woke me up and she didn't say a word; just took the coat and packed it in a dustbin liner and stacked it by the door with the other things, her lips pinched in a tight line. Then she slammed the broom cupboard door shut, and sent me upstairs to get dressed.

Well, it was like that now. Like having Dad's coat in my arms. I could feel the presence of him—Jesus, that is, not my dad. I could feel the roughness and the manhood and the courage of that great love, feel the kindness of it holding me. It didn't bring back Kathy—or Dad. It didn't stop the ache of misery inside me, but I felt different. His brokenness met my brokenness. His grief matched my grief. He understood. He was there. He knew. I could sleep.

During the next few days, I read the book the Gospel Hall people had given me. I didn't understand all of it, but there was one bit that stuck in my mind. It came near the end of the story, the last night; the night he was arrested.

He knew he had it coming, and he had a meal with his friends, a special get-together. Reminded me of the night we all went down the Bull's Head for the last time before Andy moved up to Newcastle. They didn't have draught bitter and pork scratchings at Jesus' party, but they had some kind of a meal, and after supper they passed round a cup of wine and a loaf of bread; shared it out between them. I got the impression his mates didn't have a clue what he had coming to him, but he knew all right; because he said the wine was to be his blood, and the bread, he said, ripping it apart in his hands, was his body.

He said, 'Do this, in remembrance of me.' It didn't seem much to ask.

When Thursday came, I went to the house in Flanders Road, no. 48. When I saw it, I almost turned round and went home. The long gravel drive led through a garden, stacked out with bushes and flowers like the Parks and Gardens Department, to a house that could have picked our house up and put it in its pocket. They had two cars parked in the open garage: a big, flash Audi and a little Citroen 2CV. You could have fitted two people in bed watching telly on the front porch, and the front door had a stained-glass window. I wondered whatever sort of people lived here. I rang the bell.

My doctor opened the door. Well, that was interesting. He didn't recognise me, but he seemed pleased to see me when I explained that the Mission Hall people had sent me after their meeting last Sunday. He introduced himself (still not recognising me) and he told me to call him Michael, but I felt a bit uncomfortable with that, and I called him Dr Robinson when I had to call him anything. It was the same with his wife. I called her Mrs Robinson, although she said to call her Susan.

The inside of the house lived up to the outside. They showed me into a room where some people were sitting in easy chairs grouped around a huge glass-topped coffee table that stood on a white fur rug. I sat down beside a lady on their pale pink leather sofa, and looked at it all in amazement. On the sideboard a collection of weird carvings from Africa or India or somewhere stared at me, and above them on the wall hung an enormous painting of a woman kneeling down. She had a skirt on, but her breasts were naked. She was bright blue.

It wasn't really what I'd expected. My mum would have half-killed me if I'd stuck a picture like that on the wall. The carvings were worse. Some of them were men.

They weren't my kind, really, the people at the nurture group. County types, mostly. I felt a bit ignorant, to be honest, but they were very friendly. We had chocolate biscuits and coffee in little cups with saucers, and I waited nervously for the nurturing to begin. Then a girl called Jill picked up a guitar and they sang some songs. I didn't know the songs, so I sat quiet, a bit embarrassed, while they sang.

After the singing, they all got out Bibles, except me, because I didn't have one. Dr Robinson lent me his. He asked me if I had one at home, and when I said 'no', he said I could keep it. They started a discussion and kept looking up quotations in the Bible. They all knew where to find everything. It was amazing. Someone would say something like, 'Oh, that's Galoshes fifteen!' and they'd all go thumbing through and find it right away, while I was left looking sideways at the Bible of the lady next to me, trying to see the page number. It said page 259, but when I looked up page 259, it was a completely different story about a bloke called Joshua, and I felt stupid and didn't want to say I couldn't find it.

After the Bible, we had prayers. They didn't use books for that, just bowed their heads and took it in turns to say a prayer. I sat looking at the white fur rug and Dr Robinson's natty grey shoes with little gold chains on them. I looked down at my beat-up old trainers, and I wished I'd asked Mum to wash my jeans.

The lady next to me was saying, 'Thank you, Jesus, for dying for us. Thank you for bringing Trevor to share with us. Thank you, Jesus, for dying for Trevor.'

I didn't know how it could be, in that padded, posh, expensive house, but it was right there with me again: the crash of the hammer, the convulsion of pain of the man on the cross, who loved us enough for that. And he was there, and the feel of him, the goodness and the peace, the rough manhood, was more real than the fancy settee I was sitting on, or the fitted carpet, or the china cups on the glass table. But—dying for me? I suppose, if he died for all of us, then he must have died for me. Whatever that meant.

I took Dr Robinson's Bible home with me that night, and I had a look through the index in bed before I went to sleep. It had my Gospel of Luke in it, and there was a Gospel of Matthew as well, and two more. I flipped through the New Testament part of the Bible, and there it was again: 'Do this in remembrance of me,' in a book called 1 Corinthians.

'Do this in remembrance of me.' I'd privately thought I wouldn't go back to the Robinsons' house, although they did say, 'Oh, do come next Thursday,' but it seemed as though I should. 'Do this in remembrance of me,' he said. If that was what he wanted, it seemed little enough to do.

So the next Thursday, I bought a ring-pull can of red wine from the supermarket, and one of those little Hovis loaves, and I took them in a carrier bag, along with Dr Robinson's Bible, to the meeting. I waited till the songs were over, then I got out the bread and the wine and put them on the table, in among the empty coffee cups and saucers and the half-finished plate of biscuits.

'I've been reading the Bible you gave me, about Jesus. It says he said, "Do this in remembrance of me." I've brought some bread and wine so we could do it like he said.'

It had seemed simple enough, but fools rush in where angels fear to tread. Jill, the girl with the guitar, said very quickly, a bit breathless, 'Oh, I'm afraid I couldn't. It's got alcohol in it and I'm afraid I don't. . . .'

And Mrs Robinson said, in the tone of voice that they always call 'firm but kind' in stories, as if she was talking to a little kid, 'That's a lovely idea, Trevor, but I don't think we can do it just like that. You see, the host has to be consecrated by a priest.'

The host? I looked at Dr Robinson, a bit puzzled. 'The what?' I said.

'The host, dear,' said Mrs Robinson. 'The bread and wine.'

I felt like a real twit, because I could see I'd put my foot in it somehow and it just wasn't on. I didn't know anything about any priest—it hadn't said anything about that in the Gospel—so I just put the wine and the bread back in my bag again and decided to keep my mouth shut in future.

I kept on going to the Thursday group though, in spite of everything. I got to know a bit more about it all, and I got some opinions of my own on the subject. I read up some more of the Bible, and I found out that priests finished with the Old Testament. After Jesus came, it was Jesus who was the priest, and we were all a priest together because of belonging to him too. To this day I can't make out how they can square all this priest lark. You don't need a priest to make the bread and wine holy; not when you've got Jesus right there with you.

Dr and Mrs Robinson said I should go to church if I wanted to be a Christian. I supposed I did. It had crept up on me somehow, being a Christian. I don't know that I wanted to be anything in particular, but life was different with the thought that Jesus was there with me, and I liked the difference.

So I went to church, and they had the bread and wine there, and the story of him saying, 'Do this in remembrance of me.' But somehow, the way they did it—the vicar in his robes and all those prayers and mumbo-jumbo—made me feel like they were handling the whole thing with surgical gloves on in case they got germs. It wasn't what I'd thought at all. I wanted to *do* it: get in there with Jesus, rip the bread like he ripped it, like nails ripping flesh. I wanted to kneel down and give it to the man next to me; kneel in front of him to give it to him, like Jesus knelt down before his disciples on that last night, to wash their feet—'Do this in remembrance of me.'

They ran a Youth Fellowship at the church, for their own kids and for the teenagers from the other churches round about. I joined it, and it was singing and prayers and Bible-reading like the nurture group, only not so posh and stifling. I learned a lot at that Youth Fellowship; learned about the gospels and the rest of the New Testament, and some about the Old Testament too. But the more I learned and the more I thought, the more it bugged me, '*Do* this in remembrance of me.'

So one night, I tried again. I took a bottle of Mateus Rosé and a couple of slices of Mighty White up to Dave's house, where the Youth Fellowship was meeting that night. I put them on the floor among the coffee mugs and the song-books, and I said, 'It says in the gospels, "Do this in remembrance of me." What about it, then?'

I tell you, it was like déjà vu! The words were scarcely out of my mouth before Vicky said, 'I'm sorry, Trevor, I'm a Methodist. We don't have alcohol at communion.'

And Ken said, 'I'm afraid I can't do that. I'm a Catholic, and I couldn't take part in a eucharist unless a priest was there to consecrate the host.'

Well, this time I'd read it all up and I was ready for them. I asked Vicky what she thought of the wedding Jesus went to, where he turned six socking great jars of water into wine, and that was for a houseful of people who were half-cut already. I told her she was backing a loser trying to be holier than thou when 'thou' was Jesus. And then I had a go at Ken. Took him through all the scriptures; told him why his theology was rubbish, and blasphemous rubbish at that.

It all got a bit heated, and Jane and Chris pitched in with their two penn'orth while we were at it. In the end, Vicky walked out in tears and slammed the door. Ken asked me if that was what my Protestant theology led to. I didn't bother to reply. He was a spineless sort of twit whose girlfriend usually did the talking for him, and she wasn't there that night.

I left around ten o'clock, all churned up inside, taking my bread and wine with me. Dave and Sharon had said they'd join in with a eucharist even if the others wouldn't, but that didn't seem quite right somehow.

I walked through the park down to the sea, and sat down on the beach to think. I drank most of the wine, and threw the bread down for the seagulls to find in the morning. I *knew* I was right, but I had a bad feeling about it all. Unless the priest was there to consecrate the stuff! Can't drink alcohol! I drank the last of the wine and sat there glowering at the sea.

'Do this in remembrance of me.' Who'd have thought it would be so complicated?

It was as clear as a bell. I swear it wasn't the wine. I *heard* it: 'The priest must be there to consecrate the bread and the wine, to make it holy.'

And it was Jesus. Don't ask me how I know it was him, but it was. Jesus! Taking sides against me!

'But . . . *you're* the priest,' I said, stubbornly. I said it out loud, he was so real, there with me.

'And what did I do, that last night at supper?' he said to me.

'You took the bread and the wine, and you blessed it, and gave it to them, and you said, "Do this in remembrance of me,"' I said. I knew my stuff.

'In three gospels it says you broke the bread and shared out the wine to be your broken body and blood, and in St

Luke's Gospel it says you said, "Do this in remembrance of me." '

'And in John's Gospel?' he asked me. I knew the answer to that too. I knew it all.

'In St John's Gospel, you knelt and washed the other men's feet.'

It all crowded in on me at once, then. *You are my friends, if you do as I command you.* Vicky, leaving the room in tears. *Love one another.* Ken, floundering, not able to put what he believed into convincing words. *Do this in remembrance of me.* Me, pressing the point home, letting the triumph (and contempt) creep into my voice. Jane and Chris, looking uncomfortable. *Now that I have washed your feet . . . go and do this in remembrance of me.*

And I saw how I'd shut him out. Saw how, by some ironic twist, in trying to argue and force and ridicule them into doing what he said, I'd left him right out in the cold. Made his circle of friendship into a battleground. Made the brave and humble thing he did for us into nothing more than a religious idea to argue about.

I sat there feeling like dirt, but then, I can't tell you how, I just knew he was smiling at me.

'Tell you what,' he said. 'One thing at a time. You tackle the fourth gospel, and let me work on the other three.'

Funnily enough, I've never worried about it since. I've been to Mass with Ken, and I still don't understand what they think they're doing. I've been to the Lord's Supper with Vicky, and I still can't see why they drink cough medicine out of thimbles. But as for 'Do this in remembrance of me', I know what it means now. It means being prepared to go all the way, like he did. It means putting my life into his hands and trusting that the pain of him breaking it will be a holy thing; the place where love is poured out to be shared. The place where healing can come for misery.

Coffee and songbooks, priests in robes, Ribena in perspex glasses—what does it matter? I suppose people cling to their own funny ways, but it's all so much dust and silence compared with his hand stretched out on the cross, waiting for the nail to pierce it. I defy anyone to come close enough to look at that without being broken at the memory of him. Not being the priest up at the front in fancy robes, but being the bread in the hands of High Priest Jesus, being made holy by the heartbreaking touch of his hands, of his love. Becoming the host of his brokenness, of his brave loving that gives everything, everything.

Once I'd got hold of that, it all looked different. I could *be* the host of his breaking body. He held my pain and my life in his hands, and he ripped it with the same deliberate grief. Through its dying, forgiveness and healing could flood out, like water that gushes from a broken main in the street.

He knew about Kathy, about Dad, about all my confusion and struggle. He knew, too well he knew, how much it hurt. He held it in his hands, broken bread for the life of the world. I didn't want to be broken like that—of course I didn't. But I knew I could trust him; knew I was safe in his hands. And what an honour, after all, that a man of such courage, and such amazing love, was happy to have the common bread of my life, the ordinary cup of my sorrows, and make it holy; make it into his body and blood.

A Dream Come True

What is your opinion? A man had two sons. He went and said to the first, 'My boy, you go and work in the vineyard today.' He answered, 'I will not go,' but afterwards thought better of it and went. The man then went and said the same thing to the second who answered, 'Certainly, sir,' but did not go. Which of the two did the father's will? (Matthew 21:28–31).

A Dream Come True

It is almost too much to bear, almost intolerable, to come close to another human being, the way I came close to Danny Ludlow.

There are ways—I assure you there are—of living banged up twenty-three hours a day with another man, and still maintaining intact separation: distance that preserves solitude beneath the surfaces of familiarity. It is possible to live, two lives wound intricately, inextricably round each other, yet never touching; neither life breaching for a moment its own lonely continuity. But it was not like that with Danny. From the day he walked through the cell door, his outrage rummaging the air until every atom of dust was dancing with indignation, I could not keep him out of my soul.

'They stitched me up!'

Those were the first words he spoke to me, exploding out of his magnificent sense of injustice. 'They stitched me up!'

As the door banged shut behind him, he advanced into the cell, waving his hands in agitation, forcing my complete attention with the imperative passion of his gaze, talking. Talk? I've never known anyone who could talk as much as Danny Ludlow could talk. He could talk me into a corner, talk until I wanted to hide my head in my hands, talk until, lying on my side facing the wall so he couldn't see, I would stuff the knuckles of my clenched fist into my mouth to stop myself screaming, *'Shut up!'*— because his aggrieved and offended silences were louder than his words.

By the end of Danny's three months on remand, after which they took him to court and he was acquitted, I knew every dream that man had ever dreamed, every hopeless aspiration of his crazy heart, every tall and fragile story which he pulled over his vulnerable life like a girl in a chiffon blouse trying to hide her breasts from a stranger who stares more shamelessly than she can handle. He exposed his life to me, and I, against my will, against my better judgement, watched while he forced the door of my heart, so that in the end, as Danny talked, the bleakness of his childhood made my throat ache with tears, and I could feel for myself the exaltation of the trembling idiocy of his hopes, and still detect beneath them the beginnings of the familiar, unwelcome, sour taste of despair.

'They stitched me up—it wasn't me! I never did that house! I was nowhere *near* the place! I was in church! Don't laugh, it's true. Look, I can assure you—are you a believer?'

I shook my head that first day, still laughing at him.

'Are you sure? Some people are believers and they don't know it. I'm a believer. I became a Christian last time I was inside. Man, you've *got* to believe in Jesus. He's the best. He—my name's Danny. Danny Ludlow.'

He put out his hand to shake my hand. I looked into his eyes, bright blue beneath a shock of fair hair. Eyes that still held a flame of hope that is a rare thing to see past childhood. The eyes of a lad who had suffered, but was not quite beaten yet. I shook his hand.

'Frank Marsden,' I said.

'Pleased to meet you, Frank. Jesus, he's the good guy.

You should ask to see the chaplain. He'll tell you. You need a faith, man, in a place like this. The grace of God, it changes everything.'

'I've met the chaplain.'

I don't know why he didn't irritate me; I wouldn't have let anyone else talk to me like that. Maybe he caught me off guard. Never argue with religious people. I should have known better.

'The church is already full of liars and hypocrites. They don't need another.'

'No, it ain't like that! Listen, Frank, they're good people, them Christians. They've been good to me. You should get your act together, man; you want to become a believer. Take it from me: he's the *best* is Jesus.'

'I'll think about it,' I said. I didn't mean it, but it turned out to be true. You couldn't live with Danny and not think about it. It was like being banged up with Billy Graham.

For two weeks I listened to the story of how he couldn't possibly have committed the burglary he was charged with, and listened to his jokes, and listened to him telling me I needed Jesus. I could have stood up in court as a witness for him by the end of that fortnight. I could have become a stand-up comic. I could have become an evangelist.

'What are you in for, anyway?' he asked me one evening, when he temporarily ran out of steam.

'GBH,' I said. He looked at me reprovingly.

'GBH. That's bad.'

'I know,' I said. 'That's why I'm in prison.'

'No, but GBH is bad, man. You can't be violent if you want to be a believer. I'm not a violent man. I've never been a violent man. Course, if someone hits you, you got to hit 'em back. That's only sensible—Jesus knows that. He was a sensible man, Jesus; a tough man. Look, he was *crucified* and he took it like a man. He knew when he was beaten. He was strong enough for most things, but the Government got him in the end. The Government killed him. You can't do anything about the Government.'

I wondered what Danny's friends at church thought about his theology. He shook his head sadly over the impossibility of the Government.

'No, he was like *us*, was Jesus: a simple man; human sort of bloke. But he wasn't violent. He was never violent. Not quite violent enough, if you understand what I mean. I'd like to see them try and crucify him if I'd been alive in them days. Not that I'm a violent man. I've never been a violent man; but if someone thumps you, well you've got to show 'em, haven't you? But GBH . . . He hit you first, did he?'

There was hope in his voice. He wanted to give me the benefit of the doubt.

'No,' I said. 'He didn't hit me. He was hitting a child.'

Relief flooded Danny's face. 'Well, there you are then. You had to do it, didn't you?'

I got out my tobacco tin, and rolled a cigarette. I remembered the child's face, a mask of terror as I walked away, my legs still shaky with adrenalin, leaving his dad whimpering on the ground. I'd just lost my head. Everyone else was looking the other way. Why couldn't I have done? Everyone hits their kids. That's what kids are for. Everyone needs someone to take out the pain of their broken dreams on.

Danny was still talking.

'Nobody should hurt kids. Kids need loving. I had a bad time when I was a kid, but when I have kids of my own, I'm going to treat them right. You got kids, Frank?'

I blew a ring of smoke, a good one, and watched it float up and gradually disperse. 'No.'

'Me neither. I got no kids, but I love kids. I got a little sister, a half-sister. She's called Mel. She's great, that little kid. I love her. You *got* to love kids. Jesus loves kids. They get to you—make you love 'em somehow.'

Yes. They get to you. I remembered one day, being a

passenger in a car, going slowly down a busy shopping street. Looking out of the window, I saw a sweet shop, and a child, just a little tot, standing on the step, reaching up to the door-knob. It was as high as she could reach; she was on tiptoe on the step. Her hand was hardly big enough to grasp the knob, an ordinary door-knob, like the bakelite door-knobs in our house. The door-knob, and the soft, childish hand reaching up to open the sweet-shop door. The hand of the child on the door to Paradise. And I was in anguish for the helplessness of the child. Maybe the door wouldn't open; the handle would be too stiff. Maybe the child would be shut out, all the confident expectation ('I can do it *by myself'*) wrecked. Maybe bigger children would come along and push her aside. Maybe she would see the sweets and her mouth would water, but she wouldn't have enough money. Maybe—it happens some-times—she would choose a sweet, and have the money, but the shop-keeper would not see her, the grown-up customers not make space for her . . . overlook her. I shifted a little on my bed, the distress of it moving about inside me. It made me sweat just remembering it. Great hands, strong hands, hands under whose strength I could do nothing, were twisting me, wringing me out. I couldn't *bear* the naive confidence of the child's hand as it reached up to open the sweet-shop door. Childhood? It resonates through the emptiness in the middle of me like the wailing of the bereaved. Kids get to you all right.

'Frank? Why don't you ever say anything? You give me the jitters. What's bugging you, man? You lie there like a stiff, and you don't speak, hardly ever. Come on, Frank, tell us a joke. Make me laugh. Have you heard about the fishmonger who bought some Odor-Eaters to put in his shoes? They ate him. Got any tobacco left? I'll pay you back tomorrow. Bill Nicholls owes me some.'

After that, Danny often talked about kids. About his own childhood, spent in sleazy furnished rooms, and in children's homes and schools for maladjusted children, and borstals: a bewildering variety of institutions which had left him unable to read or write, but educated to a very advanced level in things no kid should know anything about.

'I hate nonces,' Danny said, by way of conversation one day. It was Wednesday teatime, doughnuts. We'd just had our grub, and we were drinking mugs of tea. Sexual offenders were one of the things that preyed on Danny's mind. It was the thought of men who had been found guilty of abusing children that got to him most, and among those it was the ones who had been done for the abuse of little boys.

'I hate nonces.' He got up and started walking restlessly back and forth; the door to the window, back again.

'They deserve everything they get.' He glared a challenge at me, daring me to contradict him.

'*Everything*,' he said. 'Nobody should do them nasty things to kids. I hate 'em, Frank. Nobody should do them dirty things to kids. It makes me ashamed even to think about them things. It's sick; it's disgusting. They deserve all they get.'

I said nothing.

'Don't you think so, Frank? They deserve all they get.'

'It's a bent world,' I said. 'They were raised in it.'

'Ah, no, you can't say that! Look, I'm a Christian, I know about loving people and understanding them, but I'm telling you, Frank, you can't understand them sort of people. The things they do—you don't know, it's sick, it . . . . They deserve all they get.'

He hadn't told me, not then, everything about his childhood. I knew about the fear and the beatings; about his repeated absconding from institutions that terrified him. But the other. . . . He told me later. He could talk about it only at night, when the dark (as dark as it gets with the floodlighting invading the cell) gave him some cover, something to hide in. Even then it was only by hints and inferences that he could tell about the things that had been done to him—the uses men and women's perversions had found for his childhood.

I listened, and I helped him wake up from the nightmares that destroyed his sleep.

'I hate nonces, Frank. Men like that shouldn't be allowed to *live*. They deserve all they get. Kids ought to be loved and taken care of. Kids need their mums. When I have kids, I'm going to take care of them. I am. No one'll ever touch my kids. Life's been hard to me, but I can change all that. With God's grace, I can. It'll be different for my kids. You have to love kids, don't you? I don't know how anyone could hurt a kid. . . .'

I tried to keep his words on the outside of me, but I couldn't. Against my will, they penetrated my defences, touched on wellsprings of regret and pain I thought had long ago dried up. I was a child again, eight years old, sitting trembling in a locked bathroom while my mother banged on the door.

'Open that door, Frank, and get yourself out here! Come on, you can't stay there all night.'

'Promise you won't hit me, Mam. Promise.'

And her scornful laughter, mocking my fear.

'Hit you? When you've had what's coming to you, boy, you won't know where to put yourself.'

She meant it. I knew. My screams had been testimony enough many a time.

'. . . home, it'll be safe and cosy. My girl will cook for me and make it nice, and we'll be happy together.'

He was still talking.

'. . . and our kids—they'll be happy too. A little girl, and a little boy; our own place. And I'll have a job, a good job. I'll make stacks of money . . . .'

Long after he had gone to sleep, he would leave me

wakeful, living with the echo of his helpless cry: 'I *hate* nonces!' It reminded me of the child who cries in impotent, tearful anger, 'I *hate* you, Dad!' Anger that effects no change. The powerless rage of children that effects nothing. I understood that anger—every prisoner knows the impotent fury of the powerless, the under-dog's futile rage. It was himself he hated really. Somewhere, in the ruin of his innocence, he had exchanged his self-respect for shame.

Lying in the sleepless dark, I tasted and examined my own shame, my own self-disgust. The times I had beaten Maxine, blinded and possessed by the torments of my own guilt and self-hatred. Hatred that fuelled hatred. Guilt that bred violence. Violence that left me shaken and sick with shame, hating myself for ever; for ever. Hating the sight of her bruised face that filled me with shame; hating her for being the living reminder of my violence, my guilt. She was my shame, and I hated her for it. Maxine, who loved me, who pitied my tears of self-disgust until I *burned* with shame.

I lay on the bed with my tobacco tin on my belly, rolling a cigarette, lighting it, exiled from sleep, from innocence, from love, from forgetting. I understood Danny's hatred well enough—better than he did. It helps to hate someone outside yourself. That's what nonces are for. They save people like Danny from having the last sparks of hope choked by shame.

All night I would lie there sleepless. All night. And in the morning, slopping out time, weary and yawning, Danny would be as perky as ever, saying to me: 'Here, Frank, you'd better keep your eyes open today.' 'Why?' 'Well, if you don't, you'll keep banging into things.' Anyone else, *anyone* else, and you'd have had to scrape them off the wall. But Danny—he just made me laugh, that's all.

'Did you—were you ever in love, Frank?' He had twisted

over impulsively on his bed, his eager eyes searching my silence. I felt in my pocket for my Rizlas and tobacco. I was down to the last of it. In some places that cigarette was one shred thick. You should try lighting a cigarette one shred thick with a lighter made from a lump of wood and string from a prison mop. You should try it.

'Frank?'

I had it alight, inhaled, blew a smoke ring.

'Ah, come on, Frank! Don't hold out on me!'

I don't know how he did it, that lad; how he bypassed the doors to my soul that shut other men out, but he did. I didn't know what to say. I blew another ring of smoke. In love?

'I don't know.'

He relaxed back onto his bed, disappointed.

'You don't *know*? You don't know if you've ever been in love?'

What could I say to him about love, me? I'd tried to love. Wanted to love.

'I almost got married.'

'What went wrong?' He raised himself up on his elbow, interested again.

'Everything. Nothing. I don't know.'

I closed my eyes. Maxine. She'd shipwrecked her heart on mine. We'd spent more time splitting up than being together. I remembered her face, that last day we spent together. I was in court on Monday—didn't know how it would turn out. It was to be a special day, just the two of us. A blue, sweet, June day. We took a picnic, went on a bus out into the country.

It was like all our special days: all right to begin with and disastrous in the end. We ate our picnic and made love in the meadow. I remember the larks singing, and the softness of the breeze. Afterwards, we lay quiet in the grass. I lit a cigarette. It was good—the breeze and the wordless, wild song of the larks. For once I felt at ease in my own body, at peace maybe.

Maxine was looking at me; I could suddenly feel her eyes, her attention, tiptoeing shyly into my soul. She was going to speak. I could feel her getting ready to speak. I smoked my cigarette and waited. Here we go, I thought.

'I touch you, and there is something cool, something still, a lovely shimmering between us. You, being with you, has made my soul like a house by the river, filled all day with the quivering of light reflected by the water. Cool and serene, a long vibrant note of clarity, a singing.'

Maxine was a poet. She liked words. She got her cool, still loveliness out of books and out of her own head. She certainly didn't get it from spending time with me.

She was looking at me, her face vulnerable, composed into a sort of peaceful joy, a soft, fragile radiance. I could see her out of the corner of my eye. I could see her, the gentle glow of hope and trust, the naked soul. I hated her for it. It fanned into a blaze—the fear, the wound, the isolation at the heart of me. I wanted to rage at her: 'For pity's sake, shut it up before someone sees it! Put it away! Don't have it all on show like that! Don't you know what the world will do to those who hope, who trust like little children?'

I could see, out of the corner of my eye, that shining, loving, peaceful face; and I wanted to destroy it, grab her by the hair, kick the face into a pulp, smash it, destroy for ever the trembling hope and blossoming love.

'I can't do it!' the inside of me screamed. 'I can't *be* what she wants of me. I can't give that guarantee! Stop trusting me. Stop hoping for me, you stupid, stupid . . . bitch.'

The kernel of me—the kernel of pain that throbbed and ached and burned always, the centre of me that wept for pain and loneliness even when I was most loved—flamed up and threatened to engulf me.

Very deliberately I stubbed out my cigarette on the dry,

cracked earth. With slow, concentrated violence I ground out the sparks of it; ground to bits the little shreds of tobacco and paper. Then I forced myself to raise my head, to look at her, to meet the intolerable softness of her love.

'That's wonderful,' I said with a smile.

She looked at me, her eyes lit with transparent hope and expectancy. Clearly 'that's wonderful' was not enough. Irritation and resentment itched peevishly at me, the familiar lesser pain following in the wake of my soul's agony. I tried again. 'Look, I love you. I love you . . . but. . . .'

Her radiance began to dim. The exaltation waned as the first shadows of disappointment clouded her face. I groped for words, desperately, and failed.

'You want too much of me!' I cried out at last. 'I can't— I'm not—oh, let me *be*!'

And under the anguish of her gaze I scrambled to my feet and walked back down the track to the field gate.

'I've never been in love, Frank. I've never been in love.'

I blew another smoke ring. I felt too churned up inside to feign attention. Besides, there was no need to look interested. Danny would talk whether I was listening or not. I would fall asleep and he would still be talking. If I *died* I don't think it would have stopped him. My corpse would first be shrouded then buried in his words.

'I've never been in love. I'm shy with girls—nice girls. All the girls I've had have been, you know, one night stands. Not girls you fall in love with. I'm going to be in love though, one day. One day I'm going to meet a nice girl, a really nice girl, and we'll get married, and have our own place; maybe even a flat—maybe even a house! I'll get a job, a good job, on the level, and give her all my money, and she can look after it and just give me pocket money, and I'll be all right then. We'll have kids—a girl first and then a boy; two little kids. We'll look after them properly, love them the way kids should be loved. No one'll *ever* do anything bad to my kids. I'll be there to protect them. And their mum, she'll be there too. She'll *always* be there. We'll love each other and we'll be happy. When I get out of here, I'm going straight, and I'm going to get some responsibilities, keep me steady. I'm going to get a good job, get some qualifications. And I'm going to find a girl. A nice girl.'

The day after that, Danny was put on the block for three days for swearing at one of the screws. Three sweet days of peace. I lay on my bed, working out algebra formulae and composing tongue-twisters, enjoying the silence. I thought about Maxine; wondered what she was doing, if she'd found someone else. It didn't do to think about that too long. I've seen men tear themselves apart wondering about that.

I wondered about Danny; wondered if his dream would ever come true. There was a ridiculous hope about him, a tragic optimism, that drew me reluctantly under the spell of its own folly.

One of the things Danny's chaplain had told him was that there must be a God, because humanity has need of a God to worship. If there is a question, so his reasoning went, it shows that somewhere in the world there are answers to questions. The fact that a man hungers tells us that there is such a thing as food.

What the chaplain didn't point out to Danny was that just because a man hungers, it doesn't mean he's going to be fed. Because he stands at the barred window looking down into the exercise yard, it doesn't mean he's going to be set free.

My own private opinion was that God had been invented by people who were hungry and were never going to be fed; people who were lonely and who were never going to be loved. The alcoholic, the broken-hearted, the street people—they *need* a God. What else have they got? Their God, so far as I could see, was the name they put

to their pathetic refusal to admit that *never* in all eternity
would there be justice, let alone mercy, for the likes of
them.

Danny would have none of this.

'It ain't like that, Frank,' he would say. 'You don't understand at all. Jesus. Jesus is the man. He's the business, is
Jesus; he's the best. He's going to kill all the evil in the
world, and we've got to help him do it. He's going to make
it right, so there'll be no more hating, and no more bad
things. He's going to make it right. You'll see. You need
Jesus, Frank. He's not far away. He's here to help us in all
this mess. He's straightened me out, for sure. He under-
stands, does Jesus. He helps me. With his grace, I'm going
to go straight. With his grace, I'm going to find a girl and
settle down. A nice girl. With his grace, we'll find a place to
live, and have kids, two little kids, a girl and then a boy,
and we'll bring 'em up right. With his grace. That's for
sure.'

That's what I mean about getting into my soul. Even
when he was down on the block, Danny's words were
still going round my head. And in spite of myself, I cared
what happened to him. It was too late for *me* now; but I
cared whether Danny stayed straight, got his girl, his kids,
family and home. By the grace of Jesus.

When he came back from the block, he looked shaken.

'Hello, mate,' he said with a grin, and started to tell me
jokes; an insane patter with a note of hysteria in it. There
was no interrupting him. I lay on my bed and smoked.
Eventually he wound down.

'Well, you ain't got much to say,' he finished up lamely.
'How about, "How are you, Danny? Nice to see you back,
Danny"?'

'Nice to see you back, Danny. How are you?'

He swore at me, and sat down on his bed. Then he got
up and crossed the room, stood gazing moodily through

the little window for a moment, came back and sat down again.

'What?' I asked him. 'What happened?'

The air was uneasy with his disturbance. I looked at him carefully. There was no mark on him, no injury. I doubted if anyone had said anything to upset him. No one stayed long enough to get a word in edgeways.

'What?' I repeated.

'Yesterday morning,' he said slowly, 'I was coming back from slopping out, and Mad Joe Drummond said, "Come and have a look at this, Danny." I went. I didn't know what it was he was going to show me. It was one of the nonces, in his cell. The door was open wide. They'd had him when he came back from slopping out; guy with a fistful of razors, one held between each finger, like this. This geezer, the nonce, he was staggering around like he was drunk out of his skull. Blood everywhere, a great pool of it. Then he fell down. I looked down at him. His face. . . .' Danny stopped, swallowed, his face shaky with horror. 'Frank, I couldn't make head nor tail of his face. They shouldn't have done that to him. You know me, I hate nonces. But they shouldn't have done that to him. Someone called the screws, and they came so slowly. They took their time. That was wrong, Frank. I don't care what he done. That was wrong.'

I looked at him, and wondered how much it would take to cauterise the roots of his humanity. How much would he have to see? How much must he endure, before all the tenderness and hope in him perished utterly? He looked back at me. There was revulsion and horror about his mouth, and shock in his eyes.

'What d'you call an Irishman with three lightbulbs on his head? Sean de Lear. What d'you call a man who lives in a pile of leaves? Russell. What d'you call a man with a seagull on his head? Cliff. What—'

'Cut it out, Danny!' I said sharply. I jumped up and

grabbed his arms and shook him. He stared at me, then he laughed. He made himself laugh.

'Behave yourself, Frank,' he said. 'I'm all right.'

I lay down on my bed again, staring at the ceiling.

'Frank.' He paused. There was a quality of stillness in the pause. It wasn't like most of Danny's pauses, which were bustling with words queueing up to be released. It was a real pause, a silence.

'I want to go home.' He said it very softly. I turned my head to look at him. He was sitting on his bed, leaning his elbows on his knees, staring down at his HMP sneakers. His head was hanging, his hands were hanging. Danny? He didn't have a home. Never had a home. The hands of Danny's childhood were all fisted to bruise him or delicate to touch him in obscene caresses that shrivelled and shamed him to the core. He'd graduated from the skimpy blankets and urine-damp mattresses of childhood to shop doorways and park benches and the sofas of friends. I looked at him for a moment.

'Yeah,' I said. 'Me too. I know.'

It was on a Monday morning at eight o'clock that Danny left for his trial. We'd said our goodbyes, because his solicitor was sure of getting an acquittal. The preacher from Danny's church was to be called as an alibi witness.

He held out his hand to me.

'So long then, Frank. Stay cool. God bless you.'

'So long, Danny.'

The screws were waiting for him in the doorway. He turned back just before he walked through.

'My brother's just opened a shop. Really? How's he doing? Six months. He opened it with a crowbar.'

Then he was gone.

I spent the rest of my sentence sharing the cell with a morose fisherman who was in for smuggling dope. It was his twelfth time inside, and he had as little to say, and as cynical a view of life, as I did. He just wanted to get his bird done as quickly and quietly as possible, so he could get out and get back to his work, which was catching fish, handling stolen goods and smuggling drugs. He hardly ever spoke at all. Living with him was like being in solitary, except in solitary no one else breaks wind.

Then my time was done, and I was released. After the first buzz of freedom, life on the outside was no picnic. Another man had moved in with Maxine, so I lived in a hostel in Bethnal Green for a while. Eventually I found a bedsit of my own, and got some work as a scaffolder.

I saw Danny Ludlow once more, and once only; in the London Underground, at Victoria. He was squatting on the ground, trying to fasten the restraining straps of a push-chair around a wriggling, struggling child. It was a baby of about eighteen months—an under-nourished, miserable scrap of whining rebellion. Danny was squinting through the smoke of his cigarette, which he had stuck in the corner of his mouth, needing both hands to do the job, one to hold down the fractious child, and one to fasten the strap. He could have done with three hands really.

Beside them, watching with a kind of bored amusement, a skinny girl with dyed hair and too much make-up lounged against the wall, her hand clutched by an older child. Both the children had a tangle of silver-fair curls, and the skin of their pinched, hard little faces was so fine you could see the blue-green of their veins.

The baby's mouth was a smudge of livid orange, pre-sumably from the half-eaten ice lolly that lay melting on the ground a yard away. A trickle of the same bright, artificial colour lay on the grubby blue of the baby's coat. Someone, long ago, had bought that coat as an impractical bit of ice-blue fluff. By the time it had been handed down to Danny's children, it was simply tawdry, matted. The older child, clothed in ill-fitting shoes and a school rain-coat, should have been a pretty little girl, but the peevish set of her mouth, and the cunning, acquisitive glint in her eyes marred that. She had a yellowing bruise on her cheek.

The baby's blindly lashing hands knocked the cigarette out of Danny's mouth. He swore, viciously, and struck the child on the side of the head. The instant he'd done it, he glanced up at the young woman, his face grimacing with anxiety. She, smirking with embarrassment, pushed away from the wall, and towed the older child off towards the steps as the baby began to scream.

The strap was done, and Danny stood up and grasped the handle of the pushchair. He did not see me, though I stood near enough to look full in his face, to see in his eyes, without any possibility of forgetting it—the weary, baffled defeat that filled his soul. He bent down and retrieved the still-smouldering cigarette. The last I saw of him, he was manhandling the pushchair up the stairway of the exit, while his child's screams echoed all around him.

I stood there a while, then I walked slowly up into Victoria Street. I walked along as far as Westminster Cathedral, and on an impulse I went inside. I sat down at the back and looked round at the polished marble, the ornate and solemn architecture. It reminded me of a tomb. That Jesus whom Danny had talked about in the smoky fug of our cell—if he was here, he must be dead. He didn't belong in a place like this.

I knelt down on the floor, but it was no use. I had nothing to say to Danny's God. I got to my feet and left the place. In the doorway a tramp sat begging, his head bowed and his empty palm silently stretched out. As I walked down the steps and across the square, through the huddling crowds of pigeons, I could see Danny's bewildered, beaten, guilty eyes; and I asked his God, 'Where are you? You, risen Jesus; you, Lord of mercy, the human and simple God. Where are you? Where is your all-sufficient grace?'

But I never got an answer.

An Invisible Woman

*It was you who created my inmost self . . .
you know me through and through (Psalm 139:13–14).*

An Invisible Woman

The Reverend Maxwell Harrison was a marvellous man. Everybody said so. A Yorkshire man, the son of a weaver and an office cleaner, he had begun his preaching days in the pulpit of a large, forbidding, red-brick chapel on the outskirts of Bradford, and never looked back. The ministry, the superintendent ministry, and now he was being welcomed as the new Chairman of District, here in the prosperous South East.

An imposing man, tall and broad-shouldered, his florid face framed by its mane of white hair beamed its confidence and goodwill with positive energy enough to make a hundred-watt lightbulb look sick. His hearty laugh rang out now in the vestry among the gathering of ordained men and church and circuit stewards as they waited the last five minutes before processing together into West Parade Chapel, the showcase chapel of the Circuit, the Superintendent Minister's chapel, where a congregation drawn from the whole district now sat in their best hats and Sunday suits, waiting to meet their new Chairman of District.

They were not disappointed. Maxwell Harrison spoke in large and convincing terms of his vision for the future of his new District, and with engaging humility on the subject of his own abilities and strengths. With a twinkle of humour in his eye, but nicely underlined by a trace of boyish earnestness in his voice, he concluded this, his first appearance before them: 'Nor can I pretend that I would be able to achieve, remember or organise anything without the faithful and capable assistance of my wife. For thirty-seven years my wife has never failed to keep me supplied with soothing cups of tea, to be able to put her hand—instantly—on all those vital pieces of paper I am frantically searching for, to take messages from all kinds and conditions of callers, and to provide a calm and stabilising influence in the hectic and high-pressure calling of the Methodist ministry. Different people show their service to God in different ways, and all of us have something special to give. It is entirely due to the vigilance and competence of my wife that not once, in thirty-seven years, has our household run out of coffee or postage stamps. I'm sure the good Lord considers her a credit to him.'

They loved him. Over tea and biscuits in the hall afterwards, they queued for the favour of his smile, his candid handshake. His manners were impeccable, but the Yorkshire accent when he spoke assured them that he was no worldly sophisticate.

The previous Chairman had been something of a disappointment. He had had to retire early because of a rather embarrassing personal problem whose nature could never be fully disclosed. His wife Elise had been an irritation too. She was a lithographer and a sculptor, and insisted on decorating the front garden of the manse with a large piece in pink granite entitled Fluid Enigma. She dyed her hair red and wore outrageous African earrings and refused to get up in the mornings. Not a suitable person at all really; not for staff at this level.

It was a relief to see the Reverend Maxwell Harrison's wife standing at his side, dressed so becomingly in a fawn angora cardigan, and a polyester silk blouse that tied at the neck in a small bow. Her feet were enclosed in the neat suede shoes of a woman who would never, under any circumstances, open the door to a Divisional Secretary at eleven o'clock in the morning, with a sherry in one hand and nothing on but a rather flimsy dressing gown. Mrs Harrison's beige tweed skirt reached to just below the knee, and was a welcome sight after the memory of the flamboyant purple silk that had flowed and shimmered round Elise on the occasion of the previous Chairman's farewell tea.

Yes, this looked altogether a most satisfactory appointment. The Reverend Maxwell Harrison was going to fit in well. The District breathed a sigh of relief.

Mrs Harrison received a warm welcome from the ladies, who invited her to the Luncheon Club, and honoured her with the presidency of the Women's Bright Hour. Two or three invitations soon distinguished the mantelshelf in the Chairman's manse, requesting the pleasure of the company of the Reverend and Mrs Maxwell Harrison, from some of the wealthier Methodists of the District. Maxwell Harrison knew a certain glow of triumph, of which he repented on his knees at his bedside. Rejoicing in personal success was not permissible for a professional Christian, but he wished Ma and Dad had lived to see him now.

The manse was situated in a discreetly well-to-do residential area, one of the slow, quiet, leafy streets in the more exclusive end of the town. Shops would have been out of place there, but it could have taken only ten minutes' brisk walking to reach the small parade of family businesses at the bottom of the hill: a very reliable butcher; an excellent baker; a newsagent where one could buy Thornton's toffee, and who also stocked a modest range of knitting wools and some equally modest ladies' paperback romances. A greengrocer eked a living out of his tired lettuces and faded courtesy beside the salon of an unimaginative and deferential hairdresser, who was happy to shampoo and set the Reverend Maxwell Harrison's wife's hair on Thursday afternoons.

During one of her afternoon visits to the hairdresser, in the course of conversation, Mrs Harrison discovered where the shoe shops could be found. She needed a new pair of navy-blue court shoes. The pair she had was rather worn, and where it might be acceptable for her beige walking shoes to be worn to the point even of comfort, a navy-blue shoe was either immaculate or unwearable, especially in this Circuit.

After lunch on the following day, Mrs Harrison deposited the greasy remains of two lamb chops in the bin, washed up the plates and set a tray for Maxwell's afternoon tea in case she failed to be back before him. She switched on the answer-phone and walked into town.

She found Waldorf Street without any trouble, and there were indeed five or more shoe shops there, as her hairdresser had promised. After comparing the window displays, she chose one shop which seemed to have the right balance of style, price and reliable make. Mrs Harrison went into the shop.

It had not occurred to her that the first week of September was not a good time to visit a shoe shop. The second of Mrs Harrison's two sons had left home five years ago, to pursue a career in the BBC. His older brother was the sales director of a plastic appliances manufacturing firm. Neither of them had married yet. There were no grandchildren. No children ever ruffled the decorous worship of Sunday morning chapel. No children troubled the peace of the neighbourhood where she lived, or carved their names on the ornamental cherry trees that lined its streets. Children were no longer a feature of Mrs Harrison's life. She had simply forgotten that in the first week of September shoe shops are a seething mass of harassed mothers and fractious children buying school lace-ups for the autumn term.

Thankful that she had had the foresight to lay Maxwell a tray for his afternoon tea, Mrs Harrison sat down quietly to wait her turn.

It was then that she made a remarkable discovery. Although she had seated herself right there in the middle of the shop, the shop assistants apparently could not see her. She waited patiently while the two mothers who had come in before her had their children's feet measured and fitted. Then two mothers who had come in after her, both of whom had boisterous toddlers, were served. Then a third woman was served. The shop assistants, as they hurried back and forth, did not look at Mrs Harrison at all. They would not look at her. She sat forward a little on her seat, and tried to catch the eye of the young women serving in the shop, but she was not able to. She stood up, waited indecisively a moment, then left the shop.

Mrs Harrison tried three shoe shops that afternoon, and in each one the same thing happened. She had no crying children. She was not demanding, or impatient; so she became functionally invisible.

Mrs Harrison felt at first annoyed then fascinated by this. It occurred to her that this could become a game. The childhood delight in stories of invisible elves and fairies might be brought into reality. Mrs Harrison wondered how invisible it was possible to be. She began to experiment. She stood placidly in the queue at the chemist while two other ladies came after her and were served before her. She watched how they made themselves visible by leaning across the counter, looking the sales assistant in the eye and thrusting towards her the shampoo and corn-plasters they wanted to buy. Mrs Harrison stood there and faded, with remarkable success. It was an effort for the girl to take her money at all.

So much for shops. But then, she supposed, the sales assistants did not really want her to be there. She wondered how it might work among acquaintances, friends, family even. She thought of all the times she had stood at Maxwell's side smiling and shaking the hands of strangers. Perhaps . . . maybe . . . they had never seen her at all. They had run an appraising eye over her clothes, her hairstyle. They had noted her demeanour, the modulation of her speaking voice, the quality of her handshake. They had found the sum of all her parts an acceptable equation. But herself . . . could it be that in some way herself had become invisible; that all the ways she expressed herself— her smile, her handshake, her dress—had become a reality in themselves, leaving her as a disembodied soul inside a shell of appearances? And if that were so, might she not simply pull up the drawbridge, become an island, entire in itself, unvisited, alone?

On Friday evening of that week, the Chairman of District had to attend a meeting organised for local preachers who were candidating for ordination. His wife went with him. She sat in one of the rows of moulded plastic chairs, watching the people arrive. A minister from a neighbouring Circuit whom she had met several times, whom she had served with coffee in her husband's manse, came and sat in her row along with two or three others. He did not speak to her, though he glanced her way, but remained in conversation with his friends for a while, until eventually their talk lapsed. She wondered if he had forgotten that he had met her; or had he not seen her? Was she to him, too, invisible, immaterial? But after a moment he turned to her. He asked her, 'And how is Littlehampton?'

She looked at him, slightly nonplussed.

'I—I don't know,' she replied. 'I live in Southharbour.'

'Oh! I beg your pardon!' he exclaimed, embarrassed. 'You're not Brian Coleman's wife, are you?'

'No,' she replied, with a smile. 'I'm Maxwell Harrison's wife.'

He returned, in confusion, to the safer ground of his friends' conversation.

There were, then, varying degrees of invisibility. One could be seen, but not acknowledged. One could be seen, but not recognised. She wondered if it were possible to be there, but not seen.

The following evening, when Maxwell Harrison came into his living room in search of his diary, his wife was sitting, very quietly, very still, in a wing chair in the corner of the room. He did not notice her there at all. He rummaged in the desk and left the room.

Mrs Harrison found that if she sat very quietly on a Sunday morning, two-thirds of the way towards the back of the church, near the wall, no one would speak to her or look at her. She practised standing still, very still, on the bend of the stairs in a place of shadows when the Reverend Harrison came in from a meeting and hung his hat on the newel post. He did not glance up. No vibration of her presence attracted his attention.

She found that if she stood immobile near the back door, he could come right into the kitchen and not see her. She found that it was possible to spend an entire afternoon shopping without a single sales assistant taking any notice of her at all.

At the Women's Bright Hour, she had to use a different approach. Quietness and stillness there stood out like a sore thumb. Camouflage was the thing there. A tireless smile and a seamless patter about baking and knitting constructed a hide in which she could shelter without ever arousing the possibility of real communication with another human being.

After some weeks of experimenting with invisibility, Maxwell Harrison's wife began to wonder if it would be possible to disappear *totally*; for her body to vanish within her husband's manse as surely as her self had vanished into his life.

She began to experiment further. When she heard Maxwell's key in the door, she would shut herself in

the wardrobe in the spare room, or slide herself under
the bed. Once, when the moment caught her unawares
downstairs, she stepped quickly into the coat cupboard
under the stairs. She would wait until he had settled
down to work in his study, then emerge silently from
her hiding place and make her way stealthily to the front
door. She would open it, shut it with a bang, and call
out: 'Maxwell! I'm home!' in a cheery voice.

The Reverend Harrison, whose work demanded a great
deal of time and concentration, felt relieved that his wife
was settling in so well, and finding so much to occupy her.

When he had gone out during the day, his wife worked
in the garden and cleaned the house, bought the essential
food shopping and went once a week to the hairdresser.
She attended the Women's Bright Hour and the Luncheon
Club, and all the time she practised being invisible. She
shopped at the supermarket, where she could complete all
her purchases, and even pay for them, without once
exchanging a word or catching the eye of another human
being. She changed her hairdresser, visiting instead the
salon at the big department store in Southharbour town
centre, where she had discovered she could stand at the
reception desk for up to twenty minutes without running
the risk of attracting any attention at all.

At the Luncheon Club and the Bright Hour, she stood
behind a veil of words, a smoke-screen of exchange con-
cerning pork chops, brands of washing powder and the
weather.

At night, she found that by calling, 'Coming up in a
minute, darling!' to Maxwell, wearied as he was with the
endless effort of maintaining the roles and façades of the
ideal Chairman, he would be sunk in sleep long before she
appeared silently in the bedroom doorway. In the dawn
light, she would look at him lying beside her, his face
sagging slack in the oblivion of sleep; and she would slip

out of bed and downstairs long before he reached out for her as the amorous dreams of wakefulness began to stir.

There came a time when she no longer felt the need of human companionship at all; could not remember if she had ever known it. She could not even feel sure that such a thing existed on the plane of reality. On the whole she was inclined to suspect that it was no more than a romantic invention; that in truth human beings were as lifeless and unreachable as empty shells on the beach that tumbled and rubbed against each other in the tide, without emotion, or arousal, or regret.

With an odd spark of excitement, the Reverend Harrison's wife decided one Tuesday morning that this was the day. Today she would disappear.

She laid the breakfast table for Maxwell while he was still sleeping, then she washed, dressed, took a novel and a torch, and retired to the wardrobe in the spare room. Later, she heard him calling her.

When he went out at nine o'clock, she emerged, dusted and vacuumed the house, ate a cheese sandwich, weeded the garden for half an hour, and was back in the wardrobe by the time he came in for his lunch.

In the afternoon she had a bath and cleaned the cloak-room, and crept under the spare room bed when she heard his key in the door. She heard him call, listen to the silence, call again.

She heard the kitchen sounds of the fridge door opening and the kettle being filled at the tap, the rattle of cutlery and saucepans, the clink of milkbottles. She could smell bacon frying and toast burning, then coffee, and with that came the sound of the dead, metallic voice of the television. Safe to creep out then, which was a relief. It got a bit stuffy under the bed; not so good long term. She came out and sat on the landing, and from there she could hear him later on as the clock struck ten, telephoning acquaintances, a fellow minister; finally, the police: 'This is the Reverend Maxwell Harrison speaking. My wife has disappeared.'

The next two days proved a little tricky, with CID in and out of the house, but she risked momentary sorties to change her novel, nip to the lavatory, help herself to a cup of coffee and some pork pie from the fridge. It was not possible for the Chairman of District to cancel all his engagements, even if his wife had disappeared. He had to go out sometimes.

For a week the Reverend Harrison's wife lived like this, nipping to the shops to buy herself biscuits and cartons of fruit juice, and going out to eat in restaurants while the Reverend Harrison was out at meetings. She kept her cheque book with her, and drew money from her own account. In the evenings, while Maxwell was at his committees, she worked in the garden. She felt confident that, since he had never done any gardening or housework of any description in all their married life, it would be safe to keep the place tidy. Maxwell was unaware that its appearance had actively to be maintained, and could no more have changed a vacuum cleaner bag than designed a jet engine.

After a week, however, Mrs Harrison came down one morning to find copies of three national newspapers on the coffee table, each with her photograph prominently displayed on the front. She turned on the television and watched the news. She was intrigued to find herself the focus of a national search. 'VICAR'S WIFE DISAPPEARS' announced the newspaper headlines.

The *Methodist Recorder*, with its discreeter tone, reported: 'It is with the deepest regret that we announce the disappearance last Tuesday of the wife of the Reverend Maxwell Harrison, Chairman of the South-East District. We offer him our every sympathy and assure him of our prayers in this distressing and anxious time.'

And there was Maxwell on the news, looking harassed,

forgetting to appear genial and confident; Maxwell with a drip of egg on his tie and a crumpled shirt.

Mrs Harrison took a collection of G.K. Chesterton essays from the bookshelves and retired to the spare room to think. Clearly she would no longer be able to visit the shops or the hairdresser. Nor would she be able to weed the garden without risk of being seen by the neighbours. Indeed it would probably be impossible to use her cheque book any more. Fortunately she still had plenty of cash. It might even be wise, at this stage, while the CID were involved, to stop using the vacuum cleaner and the television.

For the next two weeks, Mrs Harrison stayed indoors, dusting, reading, doing a little embroidery. Maxwell stayed out more and more, invited to meals as well as required at meetings. Mrs Harrison had to take care not to eat too much from his provisions in the fridge and the larder: a thin slice of bread and not much more than a paring of cheese, a scrape of margarine. Tins of fish too—Maxwell never ate tinned fish, never thought about it and would never miss it. Careful: she must be careful. She weighed herself, and found she had lost four-and-a-half pounds. She looked in the mirror. Her hair needed trimming.

One night, she heard the clock strike two, and stole cautiously out of her hiding place. She paused on the landing, then slid like a shadow along the passage to the bedroom where Maxwell lay asleep in their bed. It had not been made, and the sheets not changed, for five weeks. Maxwell Harrison's wife stood looking down at his unconscious face, watching the rapid movement of his eyes beneath the eyelids. She wondered what he was dreaming about. Then she went back to the spare room bed where she slept every night, rising before dawn without a sound to make the bed and steal noiselessly into the wardrobe.

'Tomorrow,' she thought, 'I must go out. I need some fresh air.'

She went out in the afternoon, dressed in a headscarf and raincoat, apprehensive, keeping her head bent, fearful of recognition. Then she remembered the minister at the ordinands' meeting, mistaking her for Brian Coleman's wife. It would be all right. The description they had of her—'a woman of medium height in her mid-fifties; greying hair, grey eyes, quietly dressed, a non-smoker'—was a description of an invisible woman. Here, she was hidden as securely as a tree in a forest. They could have arrested two thirds of the population of Southharbour on that description.

After that, she went out quite freely, eating in some of the shabbier, greasier cafés, where she could be sure to meet no acquaintances from chapel, and where she could eat a modest meal at a price that did not erode her store of money too quickly. She was even bold enough to go to the public library, where she registered herself in the name of Brian Coleman's wife. Her one fear, that Maxwell would think of employing a woman to clean the house, proved unfounded. She herself continued to dust and to clean the bathroom; and Maxwell, as she had hoped, failed to notice.

On the first Sunday in December, Maxwell went out earlier than usual. His wife knew where he was going. He had been invited to be the guest preacher at the church anniversary of a congregation some twenty-five miles along the coast. She did not expect him home until well into the evening. This meant she could cook herself something out of the freezer. There would be time for the cooking smells to disperse long before he returned.

Mrs Harrison washed the floors in the kitchen and bathroom and cloakroom, dusted through the house and, greatly daring, vacuumed the floors. She brushed Maxwell's suits, sponging a gravy stain from the front of the pin-striped one. She hesitated over the thought of ironing his shirts, but decided on caution and left them. She cooked an early lunch, cleared away all traces of her presence, glanced up and down the street to be sure that there was nobody about, and went for a walk.

She walked down to the sea. The day was mild and bright, but cold enough down by the beach to discourage most people. Mrs Harrison went down the steps by the public toilets to the second, lower promenade. She sat herself on one of the seats built into the wall there, over-looking the beach. Sheltered from the wind in the wall's curve, it felt surprisingly warm.

There was hardly anyone in sight. At the edge of the sea, where the waves lapped the shore, a little girl hopped and danced, running shrieking from the incoming wave, then chasing the retreating sea back down the beach. Two adults were with her; both men, Mrs Harrison thought, though she could not easily tell at this distance. They both stood like men, but one of them had very long hair. The two of them stood side by side, looking out across the water.

The little girl tired of her game and wandered up the beach, looking for shells and feathers. When she had worked her way up to the heavy wooden steps that led up from the beach, she climbed onto them, clambering up onto the handrail. They made a good climbing frame. They made a good ship's bridge too, and she played at being a ship's captain for a while, calling out, '*Ahoy there!*' One of the grown-ups at the sea's edge turned round and waved when she called; the long-haired one. It was a man. He had a beard.

The child swung on the railings that fenced the walkway, leaning back to gaze at the sky, her hair hanging down. She began to sing, and danced to her own singing on the prom. Suddenly, she noticed Mrs Harrison sitting quietly in her niche in the sea wall. She stopped short, and looked at her. Mrs Harrison smiled.

'Hello,' said the child.

'Hello,' said Mrs Harrison.

The child took two steps towards her. She looked at Mrs

Harrison carefully. An entire interview took place in that look. Mrs Harrison felt sure it was the most rigorous interrogation she had ever undergone. She found herself wondering if she would pass the severity of its testing.

'My name is Laura,' the child announced. Evidently Mrs Harrison would do.

'Hello, Laura,' she replied.

'I am five years old.' Laura studied Mrs Harrison thoughtfully for another moment, then asked, 'What is your name?'

Mrs Harrison hesitated. For as long as thirty years, she had only had to explain, 'I am Maxwell Harrison's wife,' and it was enough. Now a new situation confronted her. Here was someone who, if she knew Maxwell Harrison at all, would know him only because his wife had won him notoriety on the national news. But five-year-olds do not watch the news.

'I am Mrs Harrison.'

The child looked puzzled.

'But what's your name?' she said.

'Mrs Harrison,' Maxwell Harrison's wife repeated. 'That *is* my name.'

The child shook her head. 'No,' she said. 'My name is Laura. What is your name?'

Maxwell Harrison's wife understood at last.

'Rosemary,' she replied. 'I am Rosemary.'

She could hear the footsteps of the two men scrunching on the pebbles of the beach. Doubtless they were coming to investigate, having seen the child talking with a stranger.

'Here comes Philip,' said the child, her face suddenly lighting up in a smile, 'and Sam.'

Maxwell Harrison's wife watched the two men climb up the wooden steps and approach her. They were very different from each other, but their friendship was evident in the way they walked; easy together, companionable.

'This is Sam!' the child cried excitedly, seizing the hand

of the bearded man. He was tall, and very thin, his collar bones sharp even under his ragged woollen jumper. He wore extremely old and dirty jeans, and running shoes in the last stages of disintegration. His hair, tangled by the wind, was long; down to his elbows almost. Mrs Harrison took in all this, every detail spelling out a lifestyle as repellent as it was alien, but her eyes stopped at his eyes which, benign and intelligent, returned her gaze, questioning her eyes almost as searchingly as the child's look had done.

'And Philip!' The child danced up and down, impatient.

Philip had attired himself immaculately in a stone-coloured raincoat and a cravat. Underneath that he sported perfectly pressed grey trousers and a new pair of brogues. His hair, cut very short, he had combed with meticulous precision into a side parting. It shone with cleanliness. He wore a pair of glasses with the thickest lenses Mrs Harrison had ever seen. He had Down's Syndrome.

Philip smiled at her with utterly disarming warmth.

'Are you Laura's friend?' he asked.

Mrs Harrison hesitated. All three of them stood waiting for her answer.

'We have only just met,' she replied, 'but I would like to be friends. My name is Rosemary.'

'Rosemary.' Philip nodded. 'Are you all alone?'

He held out his hands to her as he spoke, and after a moment's hesitation she allowed him to take both her hands. He looked at her very earnestly, and sat down beside her. She felt uneasy, a bit afraid, and glanced up at the tall, bearded young man. He stood watching them, unperturbed.

'Rosemary.' Philip lifted his hand and carefully, gravely, traced his fingertips over the surface of her face. She sensed in his touch something so infinitely gentle, so sensitively aware, that her uneasiness gave way to wonder. There was nothing to be afraid of here. His fingertips lingered, stroking gently, slowly, the skin just below her eyes.

'Soft,' he said. 'So soft. Feel, Sam; so soft!'

The bearded man shook his head, laughing, as he stood holding Laura's hand.

'Not me, Philip. I haven't your gift for making friends.'

'Yes, yes, you *must!*' Philip got to his feet, tugged at his friend's arm, pushed him onto the seat beside Mrs Harrison.

Again, she felt uneasy. He was so close to her. She could smell him: a strong, pervasive odour of tobacco, and woven in with it a smell she couldn't identify—a resinous, herby, earthy sort of smell, slightly reminiscent of incense. She liked the smell, but didn't recognise it. She made herself look up at his face. She read an apology in his eyes. He understood her uneasiness. He was, she realised, himself shy of her nearness.

'Sam!' Philip lifted his friend's hand and guided it to Rosemary's face. She closed her eyes. The touch of his fingers on her skin, the skin under her eyes, felt different from Philip's. She had never thought before, that a man's touch is as individual and unique as his face. Sam's fingers, cold from the wind, had a tremor, a hesitancy in them. He lacked Philip's sublime tenderness, indifferent to all social convention. Simply, he was too shy.

'I'm sorry,' he whispered. 'He's always like this.'

'Isn't that soft, Sam? Isn't that lovely?'

Unwillingly, the Rosemary who lived inside Mrs Harrison admitted to herself that she did want him to say yes. She opened her eyes and looked at him. So close. She had never looked at anyone so close. Even Maxwell. When she and Maxwell made love, they closed their eyes, and the rest of the time he was too busy to look at her at all.

'Yes,' said Sam.

'Let me feel!' The child scrambled up onto Sam's knee, and placed her hand on Rosemary's shoulder to steady herself, breathing hard with concentration as her fingertips explored the skin under Rosemary's eyes, stroking down from her eyes to her cheekbone. Then Laura put her hand to her own face, feeling the skin under her own eyes.

'Mine's not as soft as yours!' she said.

'Are you all alone?' Philip asked again, sitting down on the seat on the other side of Rosemary. They were all of them so close, so near her.

'Well . . . I have a husband at home. . . .' She didn't know how to answer him; knew that somehow his words were directed to her heart, to her soul. He was enquiring about her spiritual condition.

'What's his name?' asked Laura.

'He . . . Maxwell.'

'Maxwell?' It was Sam who asked. 'Harrison?'

She nodded slowly.

'Yes. I'm Maxwell Harrison's wife.'

Philip, who never watched the news, but was acutely aware of all the nuances of human emotion, quickly, protectively put his arm round her shoulders.

'Never mind,' he consoled her.

He patted her hand in commiseration. 'Come and have a cup of tea. We're going to Sam's flat for a cup of tea. Come and have a nice cup of tea.'

'Oh, *may* I?'

Then suddenly, she was terrified at having given so much of herself away, of having asked. It seemed like an admission of weakness, and she felt humiliated by her own eagerness. But Laura had hold of her hand, and Philip's arm was around her. Sam. Sam was the link with the adult world—the one of the three of them who understood adult complexity and convention. She glanced at him, embarrassed.

'I've only got three mugs,' he said. 'If you don't mind sharing.'

Sam's flat was one room on the top floor of a dilapidated

Victorian house of massive proportions on the seafront. The dormer window in his sloping ceiling looked out over the sea, but the room had no other glory. It was cold and the floor was bare boards except for an Afghan rug so old and so dirty the pattern could scarcely be discerned any more. It had worn into holes in the middle.

An unmade bed against the wall served as seating, and the rest of the room had been furnished with an ancient sideboard which had lost the handles from its doors, and an immaculate, sophisticated stereo system. On the sideboard lay strewn a clutter of teabags, mugs, a half-empty bag of sugar, teaspoons, cigarette papers, a tobacco tin, little strips of rolled-up cardboard, crumpled scraps of tin foil, a bottle of milk, a can of baked beans with sausages, a primus stove, a milk pan . . . everything. A kettle stood on the floor, plugged into the wall.

Sam squatted down and lit the gas fire, which ignited after some persuasion, with an alarming belch of flame.

'I'll go and fill up the kettle,' he said. 'Make yourselves at home.'

They heard his footsteps, light on the bare boards of the stairs, as he ran down to the shared bathroom on the floor below.

'Sit down, Rosemary,' said Philip, tut-tutting as he straightened the bed and indicated it as her seat. 'He's very untidy, is Sam. *Very* untidy.'

Rosemary sat down. Beside the bed tottered two piles of books, one supporting an overflowing ashtray. Tillich, Wiesel, Buber, de Chardin, Weil—not most people's bedtime reading. The majority of them were writers she had never heard of. She picked up a slim paperback from the top of the pile, *I and Thou*. It sounded nice. I and thou. Sam came back with the kettle, and she put the book down quickly.

'It's all right.' He had seen her. 'Borrow it if you like.'

Philip and Sam, who both took sugar, shared a cup of

tea. Laura who drank milk, and Rosemary who took no sugar, each had a cup to themselves.

'The milk isn't properly cold,' Laura said to Rosemary, confidentially, 'but it isn't Sam's fault. He hasn't got a fridge. He has to wet his socks under the cold tap and put the bottle inside them.'

'Are there any biscuits, Sam?' Philip enquired hopefully.

Sam shook his head. 'I'm sorry, Philip. I didn't forget. I'm sorry. I spent my money.'

'Mum's got some biscuits!' Laura gave her milk to Rosemary to hold, and hurried out of the room. They could hear her running all the way down three flights of stairs, and back up again a moment later, slowed down remarkably little by the climb. She burst in triumphant, two biscuits in each hand.

'One each. Mum says no more, it's nearly teatime.'

Sam played them a record. ('It's his pride and joy,' Philip explained to Rosemary, 'his system.')

'Oh! Mozart's Vespers!' Rosemary exclaimed in delight. Sam smiled at her. They were friends.

He had every right to be proud of his stereo system, Rosemary thought, as her soul lifted on the beauty of the music, every detail of it there in exquisite clarity.

Laura fished under Sam's bed and pulled out a book of fairy tales. 'Read it,' she said to Rosemary. 'There aren't any pictures, except the one on the front. Sam says I must make the pictures in my mind.'

She curled up beside Rosemary on the bed, and Rosemary read to her; *The Ugly Duckling* and *The Princess and the Pea*. All the while the beautiful music held them, built its palace of sound around them.

'I am a princess,' said Laura peacefully. 'Sam says I must be, because I can feel the lumps in my bed. Mum says it's just the springs.'

She applied an adjective of such startling obscenity to the word 'springs', that Rosemary looked down at her in consternation. She glanced at the two men, but there was no reaction on their faces, nor did Laura appear to feel she had said anything out of the ordinary. 'It probably is the springs,' (she said it again), 'but if I wasn't a princess, I wouldn't feel them, would I?'

'No,' said Rosemary. 'I suppose not.'

The music finished. Sam sat in silence, still under the spell of its beauty. Then he sighed.

'I must take you home, Philip. What time is it?'

Philip consulted his watch, frowning. Sam leaned over and looked at it.

'Half past three. A few more minutes, then we must go.'

He put the record carefully in its sleeve, and stacked it with the others against the wall. He extinguished the gas fire, and stood up to go.

'Aren't you going to wash up the cups, Sam?' Philip looked troubled. 'You'll get germs. I've told you before.'

Sam smiled. 'Later, maybe. I'm used to germs. Come on, Philip. We'll be in trouble if you're not back in good time for tea.'

The four of them clattered down the stairs, and stopped three flights down at Laura's front door.

'Bye bye, Philip.'

'Bye bye, Laura.' He stooped and kissed her.

'See you later, Sam. Bye bye, Rosemary.'

There was an air of deep reluctance about this parting. Rosemary wondered what Philip and Laura went back to. Sam opened the door of the flat and tousled the child's hair as she went in. 'Bye bye, my petal.'

'You'll walk with us, Rosemary, won't you?' Philip begged her earnestly. 'You will walk with us?'

Why not? she thought. She too felt his sadness of separation. They walked along the seafront a little way, then inland and uphill to a huge, sprawling mansion, rather down at heel, outside which a sign announced 'St Anthony's Home for Epileptic and Handicapped'.

'Go on, Philip,' said Sam. 'You'll be in trouble if you're late.'

'Goodbye, Sam.'

With extraordinary tenderness, Philip put his arms round Sam, and embraced him. Sam held him, hugged him close, then gently detached himself.

'Philip. You'll be late.'

But Philip was not going to have his parting rushed.

'Goodbye, Rosemary.' He took both her hands in his, and solemnly kissed her mouth. 'Goodbye.'

'Please, Philip. You'll be in trouble if you're late.'

They watched him as he walked up the drive and in at the door. He did not look back. His epileptic and handicapped self was closing around him. He would not show them that face.

Sam shook his head and turned away. He sat down on the low wall that ran along the front of St Anthony's forecourt.

'And what about you?' he asked.

Rosemary sat down beside him, her head bent, and told him. He listened in silence. When she looked up, he was gazing at her incredulously.

'You mean you were *at home*? All that on the news, and the whole town alive with detectives, and you were *at home*?'

She nodded. He laughed and laughed. The more he thought about it, the more he laughed.

'What d'you want to do then?' he asked, eventually.

'I don't know now.'

She couldn't put it into words. The afternoon had changed something in her, called forth a new hope in her. Maxwell Harrison's wife had disappeared, vanished; but inside the dust of that role was herself, Rosemary. Rosemary, called out of extinction, out of invisibility. Rosemary, seen and touched, and accepted. Somehow it was impossible to go back to hiding in the shadows. But it was impossible to go back to being the wife of the Chairman of District, to being a shadow herself.

'I don't know.' She looked at the bearded scarecrow beside her, wanting him to tell her what to do.

'You've got lost in your life, haven't you?' he said. 'I got lost in mine too. Don't be afraid. Suppose . . . suppose I walk back home with you? Would that help? If you like, you can come out with Philip and Laura and me next Sunday. If you like.'

'Oh, *may* I?' This time her eagerness trusted him, felt no humiliation.

He took her home.

As they turned into her street, Maxwell's car pulled up outside the manse. Rosemary stopped. She had not expected him back this soon. She could feel her heart beating.

'Don't be afraid.' She felt Sam's hand on her back, steadying her.

Then Maxwell, running, running up the road towards her.

'Rosemary!' he shouted. 'Rosemary! Rosemary! Where the dickens have you been?'

Sam in Love

So tell me, Lord, what can I expect?
My hope is in you (Psalm 39:7).

Sam in Love

Most days Sam used to go to St Peter's Church Snack Bar, in the red-brick mission hall on the seedy side of town. The snack bar opened up and started serving breakfasts at 9.30 every morning, and kept going until midday, by which time breakfasts were transposed in the imagination to lunches. Last orders just before twelve, and they closed the doors at twelve, everybody out by quarter past.

In general the clients of the snack bar lived gratefully on its white bread and greasy fry-ups, or at least on cups of hot, sugary tea with as many biscuits as you wanted when the money ran out. But Sam didn't go there to eat. He went for other purposes.

He had started to visit the snack bar on a lonely, aimless October day, to get out of the rain. He recognised it at once as a place of peace. The venture had begun as the dream child of a local clergyman—a place to offer shelter from the weather for the street people and those bed and breakfast dwellers who to all intents and purposes became street people during the day. It grew beyond that first intention to become a haven for the poor in spirit and the poor in means; for the schizophrenic and the drug addict and the alcoholic; for those newly out of prison and for young

118

single mothers living in the high-rise flats, blocks of crowded isolation, desert islands piled up and squared off and set in concrete.

Ronald bought his breakfasts there, who had lost all initiative on account of his twenty-eight years' residence in a secure institution for the criminally insane.

Michael Tooley, schizophrenic, who trod the world as though it hurt his feet but wore his rags like velvet and ermine, liked to lean the gangling length of him on his bony elbows on the counter if there came a lull in the bustle of cooking and serving. He would fix one of the staff with the blue gaze of his vacant eyes, and work the putty of his pale austere face until it would release his cracked hurdy-gurdy voice, singing 'Danny Boy' and 'The Mountains of Mourne' and 'I Will Take You Home, Kathleen'. At the end of his recital, he would beseech whomever he had seized as an audience to reassure him that God had forgiven his sins and kept a place in heaven for him. Then as a sign of his soul furling and returning to its usual taciturnity, he would beg a light for his cigarette, buy a cup of tea for 5p, and step gingerly back to his seat. And Michael had been an architect.

Even on a crowded day, noise only mushroomed spasmodically. Some of the clientele looked too dazed to sustain much conversation, and others saved their energies for survival, rousing for the occasional wisecrack, or to develop a complaint about the Welfare Office into a chorus, or to tell the stories of their lives on the odd days when someone who would listen happened along. Those life stories made a fantastic patchwork. It was impossible to tell what might be true and what merely dream, especially in the context of lives whose nearest approximation to truth might in any case have been dream, so that dreams had body and vigour and colour, for which reality formed only a vague grey backdrop.

The place suited Sam. He fitted in well, people left him

alone, and he found his own comfortable niche among the temporarily unemployed and the totally unemployable. He called in on rainy days, and sat quietly in a corner, smoking and drinking tea, and negotiating the occasional discreet purchase of cannabis, which was strictly forbidden.

It interested Sam to observe that the snack bar staff had been pummelled by life into shapes as odd as their clientele. Members of the various churches of the town, many of them wore the marks of physical ill-health or mental deficiency. Some of their faces bore the deep scoring lines of the endurance of burdens too heavy to carry, and some of them carried about them the undisguisable, almost tangible aura of crippling loneliness. For these latter, the snack bar was a kind of hearth to which they crept, drawing the comfort of acceptance and company as the wage of four hours' hard work cooking and serving meals, then scrubbing the decrepit equipment and mopping the torn lino on the floor.

Sam's own life he preferred not to dwell upon if he could help it. He was not proud of it. If he reflected on his achievements and habits, he came to a sense of uneasiness which he knew from experience was the thin veiling over a profound shame. From time to time he fell into the shame, and he had never fathomed it, and it took a lot of getting out of, so he preferred to avoid introspection, and concentrated on observing other people instead.

And now there was Eleanor.

Let that stand as a paragraph all its own, because Eleanor came as one of those slow-wheeling moments when all the blur of life freezes and the world turns in hush amid the singing of the spheres. And, oh, when first Sam saw Eleanor, he drew on his cigarette in absent-minded habit, then his hand took it from his mouth like a dreamer, stubbed it sightlessly on the ashtray, and he felt the whole of his being move like the swell of the sea in recognition and longing, all of him saying, please,

please: please notice me; please see me; please love me, touch me, know me. That tide broke on the rocks of reality, with Sam in it in a most vulnerable state, and he grazed and stunned and choked himself on the remembrance of his appearance, his categorisation in the environment of the lost, probably even his smell. When he rolled another cigarette, his hands were shaking, and that irritated him.

Sam was not unfamiliar with compassion, though he avoided the ache of it when he could, but could watch most people calmly out of the tranquillity of his disillusioned mind. A few—Philip, Laura, Rosemary—lodged in his heart; but Eleanor . . . Eleanor had him by the guts and every move of hers tugged him like an umbilical cord.

He sat motionless, that first day, watching her. Insecurity and fear and rage ground around inside him as he observed that a lot of other people found Eleanor well worth watching too. This was not surprising, for Eleanor incarnated the beauty of a summer day. Her hair, the colour of ripe corn, she twisted back from her face in a long thick plait, to work in the kitchen, so that only curling wisps and tendrils of it framed her soft and serious face, whose creamy pallor blushed shell pink on her cheeks in the heat and bustle of the snack bar. Eleanor, plump and slow and gentle in her blue cotton jumper and blue jeans, grey-blue eyes shining as she smiled (oh, dimples like a child's in her face as she smiles) at a muddled, unshaven gentleman of the road. Eleanor concentrating on pouring tea, her head on one side, the lamp overhead shining on the gold of her hair. Eleanor leaning dreamy on the counter in between customers, her face lighting in a smile as the door opened and Michael Tooley arrested his eggshell walk to look at her. Eleanor, stretching in a luxurious yawn towards closing time.

Sam hadn't been so unhappy for a long time. Failure and inadequacy were bitter herbs to chew on, and he protected himself from that when he could, but at this moment all his insecurities had got loose inside him, rampant.

Quarter to twelve. They would stop serving tea in ten minutes. Sam felt in his pocket and could have wept like a disappointed child at the unmistakable feel of two two-pence coins, and you needed five pence for a cup of tea. There was nothing else he could say to her. A hoarse mumble of 'Cup of tea, please,' would have been his limit.

In mute suffering he sat and watched Alessandro the drugs dealer stroll confidently between the tables, spread his hands on the counter so that he leaned over her in a proprietorial and suggestive kind of way, flash the white teeth of his smile at her and drawl his request for a cup of coffee. Coffee, not tea; tea was not sophisticated enough. He was too damn flashy for tea, and he had the money for coffee.

Sam hated him, swore at that moment that he'd never buy so much as a tenth of an ounce off him again; but then he saw that Eleanor didn't care for him much either (and women fell over themselves for Alessandro, though granted most of them were junkies). She stepped back a little, and wouldn't meet his eyes, and her smile was a little distant, her gaze a little oblique as she heard his request (or was it an offer?), gave him his change and his coffee. Her whole being said a polite 'no, thank you', and Alessandro lounged back to his seat with his suavity faintly tarnished. Seven pence laid out on coffee to demonstrate his wealth (comparative) and sophistication (absolute), to no avail. That would nettle him, Sam knew.

The brief satisfaction of Alessandro's rebuff froze as the possibility dawned on Sam that the same thing would most likely happen to himself. Something wild and star-tling and agonisingly alone howled like a demon in the chasm of his insides at that prospect. But he silenced it abruptly with the common sense recalling that he would not expose himself to that rebuff, because in the first place he would never lean his hands on the counter and leer suggestively at any woman—he had an understanding of human dignity and respect if he didn't have much else. And in the second place, in the case of this particular woman, all he would be able to produce would be an inarticulate mumble. Close to her, his gaze would be riveted to the floor, and his throat would close in palpitations.

Then it was gone twelve o'clock, and he had to go, and the door shut behind him. His soul lingered, wanting to stay with her. They shut the door, and he got his soul trapped in the door. It hurt worse than trapping your fingers: all of him aching to stay with her, in case she was only helping out for the one day as a favour to a friend; in case she never came there again.

The next day he came, and she was there. And the next, and the next. On a day in late June she had appeared, and every week-day that summer Sam spent his mornings in the snack bar watching her, adoring her from across the room, discovering every inflection of her voice and cherishing every little mannerism. From time to time he made a half-hearted attempt to armour his heart and regain the safety of independence, stay away for a day, but half an hour's drifting always took his feet back to the mission hall, so that he simply washed up on the doorstep at 10 o'clock instead of 9.30.

Sam wondered why on earth someone as whole and healthy and apparently unscarred as this girl wanted to spend time in the church snack bar. He puzzled over it some time before he realised that this being the university holidays Eleanor was probably a student, filling in time with voluntary work. And that was the day he heard her name for the first time: 'Eleanor, is there some bacon in the freezer? Would you look and see please, dear?'

Eleanor. Eleanor. Sam would scarcely admit even to himself that in the silent dark of two o'clock in the morning he pulled the pillow from under his head and hugged it close against his body, and whispered her name, and wanting her ached and suffered inside him so that he had to lie still, still, just to bear it.

By the end of August, Sam could not imagine life without Eleanor. The tattered moth of his life fluttered in circles around the flame of her presence, and away from it everything else belonged to darkness.

Afternoons he would sort through the morning's assortment of his memories like a child with a button box: the little frown that appeared when she grew weary, the free, happy sound of her laugh, the way she ran her fingers through her hair, uncertain, when a drunk or aggressive customer was giving trouble. She need not have worried. Sam would have defended her against armies of psychopaths, saved her from the predatory sexuality of Alessandro, given his life to shield her from hurt. And he frequently did, as he drifted in daydreams, lying on the summer beach, or walking on the hill.

Saturdays and Sundays the snack bar did not open. Sundays it stayed shut out of righteous piety, and Saturday because—well Saturday was to the world what Sunday was to the church: hectic.

Saturdays, Sam lay on his back and suffered. He saw Eleanor's face, he heard Eleanor's voice, he saw Eleanor's name unfurling in ornate script on curling banners. His memory lingered and hovered over pictures of Eleanor pouring tea, Eleanor frying eggs, Eleanor refilling the teapot, Eleanor trying (and failing) to add up the sum of three clients' breakfasts, Eleanor serving baked beans, Eleanor emptying ashtrays . . .

He read Shakespeare: 'O, wilt thou leave me so unsatisfied?' He read Barrett Browning: 'How do I love thee, let me count the ways. . . .' He read Donne: 'If ever any beauty I did see, which I desir'd, and got, t'was but a dream of thee. . . .'

One Saturday in early September, he lay reading Ben Jonson: '. . . oh so white, oh so soft, oh so sweet is she . . .' and this last book he threw on the floor, muttering, 'Oh *God*, this is going to drive me crazy!' A long while then he lay quite still on his back, wearily bracing his soul against the turmoil of hopeless hope, delightful misery, until he could stand it no longer and flung out of the flat, ran down the stairs and out of the house, walked and smoked and walked until dusk.

Then in the twilight, he was wandering back in the direction of home along the promenade, and he paused to read the brightly coloured bills outside the theatre, advertising coming productions. *Twelfth Night*. There, among the Wrestling Matches and Children's Ballet School performances, the Adults Only shows and Country & Western concerts, was a poster advertising the Royal Shakespeare Company, performing *Twelfth Night*, here in this dead-end provincial town. Sam blinked, and it was still true. Furthermore, he hadn't missed it—it was on this Friday, one night only. Friday he drew his invalidity benefit. If he booked by telephone, he needn't pay for his ticket until he picked it up. Tickets £11.50. A daring, terrifying, raggedly hopeful idea began to form in Sam's mind. It kept him awake all night.

Sunday he was rude to Philip and impatient with Laura, silent and moody. Rosemary, who spent most Sunday afternoons with the three of them now, tried tactfully to draw him out, but without success. Philip observed sagely that he thought Sam was sickening for something, and recommended him to try Beecham's powder, or gargling with salt water.

'I gargle with salt water every morning, Sam. Keeps the germs away. Every morning, after I've cleaned my teeth, Sam. Sam, you're not listening, Sam.'

'That's a very sensible precaution, Philip,' Rosemary intervened. A glance at Sam told her he was miles away.

She sighed, and wondered what was bothering him. He'd not been himself all summer.

Monday he was outside the snack bar a quarter of an hour before opening time. Eleanor arrived carrying a plastic supermarket carrier full of groceries, in the company of a shapeless green gabardine church lady topped with a limp grey perm. Eleanor, seeing Sam, smiled at him and stopped to say hello, while her companion burrowed in the depths of her maroon nylon shopping bag for the keys.

Eleanor liked Sam; liked the quietness of his hands and the steadiness of his eyes, and the sudden warmth of his smile when she came to clear the ashtray on his table, or when he thanked her for his cup of tea. She was pleased to see him. Some of the snack bar customers still made her a little afraid, but Sam felt like a friend.

Sam, paralysed by her proximity, could scarcely nod a return greeting, let alone smile. His intellect scolded him: 'This is ridiculous!' His soul knelt before her among the fag-ends and pigeon droppings, and kissed her feet. His heart danced and sang to be near enough to smell the fragrance of her hair, gaze at the texture of her skin. Only the outward shell of him leaned unmoving and silent against the wall, ragged and withdrawn, a creature of the outside. Eleanor went in, shutting the door, glancing at him with a little smile of apology. She didn't like shutting people out.

At 9.30 the snack bar opened. From 9.30 until nearly noon Sam sat in torture, rehearsing what he had determined to say to her. He had all morning, but he couldn't do it: couldn't get up from his table in the corner and cross the room to speak to her. She came to his table to clear away his empty mug, tip out the ash and cigarette butts from the ashtray into the bin, and she smiled at him, but he couldn't speak. He sat there and couldn't make himself frame the words; just looked at her and loved her, and couldn't even smile.

And midday was closing time. The doors would be closed at ten past, everyone out by 12.15.

At seven minutes to twelve Sam got to his feet like a man going to his execution. He felt dizzy and sick and terrified. All the strength seemed to have drained from his body, he had a weird feeling in his arms and neck, and his chest hurt him. Eleanor, who had been wiping down the counter, tossed the dishcloth into the sink and picked up the teapot to pour the dregs down the sink. But as she turned, she saw the expression of utter desperation on his face, and put the pot down again, waited at the counter for him, watching him with some concern.

Like Alessandro, he leaned both his hands on the counter. Unlike Alessandro, he did it not to dominate, but to support his weight because his legs were shaking.

He looked at her. 'Are you all right?' she asked him, anxious.

The grey church lady heard her. The lingering customers in the snack bar heard her. If by his own volition Sam could have ceased to exist, he would have chosen this moment. He looked at her, and he was so scared he could hardly see. Her face floated before him, isolated in a sea of fizzing black.

'W-w-will you come to the theatre with me on Friday?' he mumbled.

Eleanor stared at him in total amazement. 'What?' she said, blankly.

Sam lifted his hands from the counter and pressed his fingers to his temples, closed his eyes.

'*Sam Rowley, you are a no-hoper*!' The kindly contempt of his schoolteacher.

'*People like you are the flotsam and jetsam of society. You make me ashamed.*' His father.

'*We are finding it difficult to locate this client's particular gifting on first interview. Perhaps arboreal surgery*?' His careers consultant.

'*No.*' His bank manager.

'*No.*' The job centre.

'*I'm sorry, sir, we can't serve you here.*' Landlord of the Royal George.

'*Sam, your hair smells funny—a bit like Nan's dog.*' Laura.

'I'm sorry'—this was Eleanor—'I'm not sure I heard you correctly. What did you say?'

There is a form of desperation which emerges as a sudden saving clarity in a lost situation. It can only be found off the edge of the world, where nothing grows or sings; a place bereft of advice or common sense or technique or self-esteem or hope. Sam opened his eyes, lifted his head. He rested his hands simply on the counter, and spoke to Eleanor with the clarity of that desert.

'I am not mentally ill. I am not dangerous. I know I look a mess, but I am a human being. I said, "Will you come to the theatre with me on Friday?" because the Royal Shakespeare Company are touring with *Twelfth Night*. Please. It would save me blowing my money on dope and tobacco. I . . . please.'

Eleanor looked very hard at Sam. Having said what he had to, it was easy enough to look back at her. That searching look, examining every corner of his soul, testing his integrity, weighing his honesty, he endured almost every Sunday from Laura and Philip anyway.

'OK,' she said, to his utter amazement. 'What time?'

'Seven o'clock. On the seafront, by the newspaper kiosk opposite the theatre.' He said it quickly, afraid she would change her mind.

Eleanor nodded calmly. 'OK.'

It had never before been in Eleanor's power to place into someone's hands a gift of pure happiness. She had been well aware of Sam, observed his quietness and the shyness which gave him an almost Red Indian dignity and reserve, but she had never seen him radiate joy like this. His face, lit up in a sunburst of delight, made her laugh, happy at his happiness, dismissing her alarm at what she'd just agreed to.

The rest of that day, Sam walked in joy.

He thought he might stay away from the snack bar for the rest of the week: not make himself too readily available for Eleanor to cancel the arrangement. By 9.25 on Tuesday morning his resolve began to weaken, and at ten o'clock he was walking through the door.

Eleanor looked up as he walked in. Their eyes met. She smiled at him, for him. She had been waiting for him, looking for him. Sam could see it in her eyes. Even before he had the chance to return her smile, some central reality of him irresistibly streamed out to her. 'I'm hooked,' he thought. He thought it with contentment, but he was afraid too. With people like himself, people of the outside, Sam found himself at home; but Eleanor seemed definitely an inside person. He could detect not a whiff of anguish or despair about her anywhere. He did not want to infect her with his own, and he was also scared that her light might prove incompatible with his darkness.

'This could end in tears,' he reflected.

The old instinct to protect himself, to construct a shell of defensiveness, rose strongly, but he had learned better than that from Philip, and from Laura. The choice of remaining vulnerable reduced him to a state of panic, but there were no other viable options in a friendship.

'Tea, two sugars,' said Eleanor when he stood across the counter from her. 'You shouldn't take sugar,' she added severely. 'It'll rot your teeth, even if it doesn't make you fat.'

Sam nodded. 'Tea,' he said meekly, 'no sugar.

'If I don't have any sugar, I'll be hungry though.'

As soon as he'd said it he wished he hadn't. The nurturing instinct had deep roots in Eleanor's being, and she looked at him sharply.

'You've got no money?'

Sam said nothing. He gave her his 5p for the tea, automatically reached out for the sugar, then remembered not to.

'You've got no money?' she repeated.

'Friday. I draw the dole on Friday.'

'What will you eat till then?'

This was awful. Her questioning had the persistence of a terrier, as bad as Laura.

'I'm OK. I've got a few cans at home and . . . oh, you know. If you hang around at the end of the market, there are fruit and vegetables dropped, and . . . I've lived like it a long time. I'm OK.'

'What do you spend your benefit money on?'

Sam smiled, amused by her bluntness. She was making him uncomfortable, but he preferred it to the masked ritual of some conversations.

He shrugged. 'Books. Music.'

'Tobacco? Dope?'

'Yes, and that.'

'I wish you wouldn't.'

Sam looked at her.

'I'm sorry,' she said quickly. 'That was a very interfering thing to say.'

'I wish I wouldn't too,' he said. He smiled at her. 'Tea, no sugar. Food, no dope.'

Two other men had made their way to the counter, and stood waiting their turn. Eleanor moved to serve them, then paused.

'I don't even know your name,' she said.

'No. I'm Sam. *Now* I'm Sam. Looks like I'll be someone else by the time you've finished with me.'

She laughed. 'It's Sam I'm going to the theatre with on Friday.' Then she turned her attention to the two men waiting behind him. But she had given him a little kiss of warmth in those words, and he stowed it carefully in his heart.

As he sat sipping the hot tea, which had an unfriendly austerity about it without the sugar, he turned over the conversation in his mind, like Laura examining a treasure of shells and stones after a morning on the beach.

Sugar gave you bad teeth. Tea, no sugar. Tea didn't do much for teeth either. Stained them. Water, no tea. Dope fogged your mind, wasted your money. Eleanor wished he wouldn't. Tobacco, no dope. Tobacco stained your teeth and made your breath smell foul. No sugar, no tea, no dope, no tobacco. Water. Water . . . water . . . better have a bath. ('Sam, your hair smells funny—a bit like Nan's dog.') Better wash his hair.

Sam looked down at his hand resting on the worn red formica top of the table. His fingernails needed cutting. The sleeve of his jumper was dirty. He looked down at the rest of himself. The whole of his jumper was dirty. Jeans even dirtier.

'Now I'm Sam,' he thought, 'and the dirt is my dirt, and this is me. And she said "yes" to me dirty. But if I get cleaned up, maybe I'll still be Sam. Maybe I'll be more Sam clean. Maybe I'm two of us: dirt and Sam. Maybe for Eleanor, interacting with Sam would be nice, but not interacting with dirt. Love me, love my dirt. Hi, I'm Sam. This is my dirt; he stays with me. I use him to replace my lost confidence—dirt, not hurt. If I—if I ever—if maybe one day—suppose—if . . . if I kissed her; she's clean, smells good. She . . . I don't want to smell like any dog. And if I kissed her . . . how would it be for her to be joined at the mouth with bad teeth and bad breath, tasting nicotine and tannic acid?

'What does she taste of, then?'

The erotic possibility of this line of thought suddenly ran through Sam's body in quick fire, and teased his thinking in terror and delight.

'I'm not sure I want to taste of toothpaste either. But I do want her to want to kiss me. Oh, God, yes I do.'

With habitual caution Sam reminded himself sternly that Eleanor looked upon him as a social reject needy of kindness, and as such was highly unlikely to want to kiss him on any terms. But he thought he'd have a bath, and wash his clothes.

Meditating on this a little further, the remembrance soaked into him in slow horror that although there were two bathrooms in his house—one on the floor below him and one on the floor below that—neither bath had a plug. The inhabitants of the flats and bedsits in that house bought their own plugs, and knew better than to lend them.

He had no money till Friday. If he washed his clothes Friday, they wouldn't dry in time for Friday night. If he paid for theatre tickets and bought even a bit of food, enough to get by, and toothpaste, and a toothbrush, and soap, the launderette would be too expensive.

Sam froze in misery; cold waves of anxiety and inadequacy pulsing through him. He soaked in dismal, familiar defeat, searching his mind feebly for a possibility, a fairy godmother, a—Rosemary!

The hill up to Rosemary's house slowed Sam down a little. Well, it was not the hill so much as old fear of encounter. Was it impertinence to call at her home? Did his request go beyond the bounds of what their relationship allowed? If Rosemary had gone out and he found only Maxwell in, what could he say?

He hesitated a full minute on the doorstep before he could bring himself to ring the bell, and then he snatched his hand back as if the thing had burned him, but too late, the buzzer had sounded.

Maxwell opened the door, and eyed Sam cautiously.

'Yes?' he said, wary.

Sam realised that Maxwell had not recognised him at all, and was trying to decide whether to categorise him as vagrant, beggar or thief. He had long grown accustomed to bearing the suspicious scrutiny of strangers, but this particular venture had exhausted the reserves of his audacity already. He was able to stand his ground and bear Maxwell's distrust, but words fled his mind.

Maxwell's face, ruddy above the white dog-collar and grey clerical shirt, creased in a quick frown of impatience. One hand still held the door handle firmly, but the other he now ran through his thick white hair in exasperation. Two telephone calls had already interrupted his first twenty minutes of sermon preparation, and no sooner had he replaced the receiver than the doorbell had summoned him to this silent ragamuffin who no doubt intended to presume on his goodwill as a man of God.

'Want something to eat?' Maxwell asked him brusquely. 'I'm not going to give you any money.'

'No, thank you.' Dignity, education, sanity—all apparent in these three quiet words—caused Maxwell to look at him a little more closely. The frown deepened in perplexity and then his face cleared in recognition.

'Oh, Lord, yes, you're . . . um . . . you're—*Rosemary*!' (This last bellowed over his shoulder into the depths of the house.)

It all took too long. By the time Rosemary, tidily dressed in beige ladies' slacks and a neat grey sweater, had greeted him with surprised pleasure and welcomed him into her living room—'Sam, do make yourself at home while I get you a cup of coffee'—any remaining shreds of confidence had evaporated entirely. He had never until this moment considered his flat as anything but home; a bed, a fire, a roof, a place of music and friendship and refuge. But now, in the restrained and spotless environment of Rosemary's living room, he felt ashamed; of his appearance, his home, everything. Most Sunday afternoons she came from here to the undeniable squalor of his flat. Last week Laura had wrinkled her nose in disgust as she walked through the door—'Sam, I think you need some new trainers.' Whatever must Rosemary think?

'Is anything wrong, Sam?' She carried in the tray of coffee; sugar in a sugar bowl, a plate of biscuits.

'I mean,' she added, 'I'm pleased to see you. There doesn't have to be anything wrong. Did you just call by?'

Philip and Laura never meditated on honesty. They never perceived themselves as being honest, or consciously valued the truth. They simply saw through or turned away from all subterfuge and hypocrisy with sure and sensitive instinct. For Rosemary and Sam it was different. They clung to honesty to save them from the subtle deceits which had tangled around their feet and bound their mouths and been the root of too much unhappiness. When the four of them were together, honesty laid the foundation of their friendship. Without Philip and Laura there, Sam found himself telling a lie.

'No,' he said. 'I'm OK.'

And with that they could have entered on a dodging, feinting game: Sam protesting there was nothing amiss, while the trouble in his eyes and the hunch of his shoulders said everything was wrong. Rosemary could have pressed him to tell and he could have refused to tell her, in the tone of voice that begged her to ask again. Instead of that, Rosemary sat down and sipped her coffee and waited. She waited a long time.

She had placed Sam's coffee, and the biscuits, and the sugar beside him, on the middle-sized table from her nest of tables. Now that was a hard choice. He could either drink it—and it smelled good—or leave it there. People who have nothing wrong with them drink their coffee. People who have said there is nothing wrong, when everything is awful, have to leave their coffee to get cold until someone lets them off the hook by saying, 'Why aren't you drinking your coffee?'

Rosemary was having none of this. It had taken courage

and heart-searching to break free of social ritual and stereotypes, and she didn't want them back.

Eventually she said, 'It will be all right to sulk and drink at the same time.' And she added, softly, 'No games, Sam.'

He picked up his coffee, hesitated over the sugar, and began to drink it.

'Have a biscuit if you'd like one.'

'Um, no thanks.' He put the cup down. 'Rosemary, may I use your bath?'

In the silence that followed this request, he hung his head, miserable, ashamed. Responsible people organised themselves to own baths—or at least to own plugs so they could use rented bathrooms.

'Cut your hair, get a decent job, stop sponging off hardworking taxpayers.' His father.

'You ought to be ashamed of yourself!' ('I know. I am. Always and always.') His mother.

'Well, if you won't take the tablets, you'll just have to pull yourself up by your own bootlaces, young man.' His doctor.

'Sam. Sam, look at me.' Rosemary sounded upset. He raised his head and looked at her. Black and defiant and stormy his eyes, looking out of a horrid place that was no good for him, cut off from her—bars, he was looking through bars!

She hesitated, feeling her way to his trouble. 'There's no need to be so ashamed,' she said, gently. Bullseye! Thank you, Philip; thank you, Laura; for all your lessons in seeing through pretences. It had hit him in the gut at sixty miles an hour. There was no way he could reply.

'Would you like to have a bath now?' She spoke after enough of a pause for him to recover his balance.

'Um, no; Friday.'

Rosemary's face, puzzled, burning to ask questions, struggling to restrain them, finally made him laugh. He picked up his coffee, and drank it.

'On Friday . . .' he said, putting his cup down very

deliberately, slowly; fiddling with the sugar spoon in the bowl, not looking at her. 'On Friday I am taking someone to the theatre. I'd like to be . . . Laura says I smell like her nan's dog.'

This was true. Rosemary agreed with Laura. He swam in the sea, but his hair and his clothes needed washing. Rosemary nodded sympathetically.

'When you've had a bath,' she said, 'are you going to put those clothes back on dirty?'

He poked the sugar in the bowl, saying nothing.

'You must tell me to mind my own business if I'm prying. Is this a very special person? Is this something that matters very much?'

He put the spoon down, ran his finger round the rim of the cup, along the smooth curve of the handle.

'Yes,' he said.

Rosemary had heard that tone of voice before, but in other contexts. In the kneeling reverence of the Prayer of Humble Access at Holy Communion: 'We are not worthy even to gather up the crumbs under your table.' In the Marriage service: 'Wilt thou love her, comfort her, honour and keep her, in sickness and in health; and forsaking all other, keep thee only unto her, so long as ye both shall live?' 'I will.' I will. I will.

'Sam, when I first met you and Philip and Laura, I desperately needed to be touched and noticed and really known. The three of you, you did that for me. Philip and Laura did it without thinking, but you were a bit shy; and me, I was afraid to let you all come so close. Alarmed and glad and frightened and relieved. Now today, in return, here is a shy offer it might cost you to accept. Have a bath by all means. Will you also allow me to buy you some new clothes? And, if I dare, a hairbrush?'

The hairbrush made the difference. If she had offered to pay for a haircut, her help would have been politely refused. A hairbrush respected his choices. That made it different. He hesitated.

'I couldn't pay you back.'

'This is *me* paying *you* back, for what you did for me. This person—is she scruffy?'

'No.'

'Is she dirty?'

'No.'

'And had you in mind that, maybe, it might be possible to be very close to her?'

Silence. 'Maybe. I can dream.'

'Then how about you have a bath now while I put your clothes through the washer and the dryer, and then we do some shopping?'

She got hastily to her feet, seized his assent and pulled it through his uncertainty.

'I'll show you the bathroom,' she said firmly. 'When you've run the bath, you can just put your clothes outside.'

Obediently, he followed her.

'Here's Maxwell's shampoo. There's some bubble bath if you want it—just help yourself. All right? I'll be making you a bite of lunch to fortify you. Here's Maxwell's dressing gown. You can wear that while you're waiting for your things back.'

Sam's clothes just about survived washing. Rosemary wondered why he had not given her his underwear to wash. She decided she had pushed him far enough and said nothing about it.

Maxwell ate lunch with them, bread and vegetable soup, but his thoughts he left wrestling with his Sunday sermon in the study. It was an important sermon, to be preached at a special united service with a congregation of Anglicans, Methodists and United Reformed Church people. His mind was entirely engrossed in it. He nodded to Sam in greeting, but barely took in that he was there at all, let alone that he was wearing Maxwell's dressing gown.

'How is it coming along, dear?' asked Rosemary politely, as she put their bowls of soup in front of them and sat down with them at the table.

'Joy,' said Maxwell, as he reached for the butter. 'I'm going to preach on the duty of Christian joy. There shouldn't be any denominational pitfalls there.'

He spread a large helping of butter absentmindedly on his bread.

'Remember your cholesterol level, darling,' Rosemary murmured.

'Archbishop Ramsay said,' Maxwell declared through a mouthful of bread and butter, '(and that should keep the Anglicans happy—if you want to quote a living bishop you're walking on eggshells) that when you die, God will want to know only one thing of you.'

Maxwell paused and brandished the butter knife impressively at the serried ranks that sat before his imagination.

'*Did you enjoy yourself*? The one question God will ask you when you die is, "Did you enjoy the life you were given?"'

He leaned forward and glared challengingly at his invisible congregation. 'And what will you say to that? How will you answer him?'

Rosemary, who had been listening to Maxwell with tolerant attention while she waited for the butter, glanced at Sam and registered with alarm the slow flame of anger kindling in his eyes. Trouble. It reminded her of the days before her sons had left home. Clearly God's tactless question had touched him on the raw.

Sam growled, 'I'd tell him to f- '

'*Won't* you have some butter on your bread, Sam?' Rosemary interrupted him, snatching the butter knife out of Maxwell's hand.

'Darling, I think it's an awfully good idea to quote Bishop Ramsay, but I'm not sure that that particular quotation is the most helpful thing he ever said. Some people have really very difficult lives. In every congregation is someone with a broken heart. You said that to me yourself.'

Maxwell tucked his napkin under his chin and frowned at his bowl of soup.

'Not joy then, you think?' He made a moody beginning on the soup. 'But I'll have to start all over again! What else is there that's safe ground for a united service? Scriptural holiness? No, too Methodist. The power of the cross? No, too dicey on theories of atonement. How about Christian service in the community? No, they might think I'm being political. How about, "There abide these three, faith, hope and love; and the greatest of these is love"? I suppose faith is out of bounds for an interdenominational service. Hope and love, though? I could quote Péguy. No, maybe not, he was Catholic. That would really set the cat among the pigeons. Which church do you go to, young man?'

'I'm a spiritualist,' said Sam.

'Pardon?' Maxwell gave Sam his full attention for the first time.

'Stop it, Sam!' said Rosemary, sharply. 'He's only teasing you, darling. Eat up your soup before it goes cold.'

Sam was not happy in a department store.

'Where do you usually buy your clothes?' Rosemary had asked him, as she slotted her change into the car park ticket machine. He looked at her, sidelong.

'Oxfam,' he said.

In the shop he was uneasy, embarrassed to be spending her money, hating the air of affluence, the bustle of consumerism, the rich scent of expensive French perfumes and cosmetics that drifted through to the menswear department.

'I don't think I can hack it,' he muttered, pleading.

'Don't be so silly.' Rosemary spoke firmly. She had the same trouble with Maxwell. The only things he could purchase unaided were clerical collars and fish bait.

In the end she managed him into the purchase of a pair of jeans, a pair of jogging trousers, three T-shirts, a warm jumper, two sweat shirts and a hairbrush.

'Now is there anything else you need?' she asked him, as they stood in the queue for the cash-desk—she with her arms full of clothes, Sam with his hands dug in his pockets.

'For goodness' sake, don't be afraid to say.'

She looked at him. He looked back.

'What, Sam? Is there something else you need? Heavens, I never knew *anybody* so ridiculously bashful! What?'

'Well . . . I haven't got any underwear.' This mumbled in the direction of the floor.

'Oh, Sam! And socks too? No? Go and find some. I'll stay in the queue. Get enough, now.'

He came back with three pairs of underpants and two pairs of socks. She sent him back for the same again.

They emerged from the department store with a sense of victory. Rosemary unlocked the boot of her car in the car park, and Sam loaded in the bags.

He stood beside her as she shut the boot, then gently took hold of her arms, and turned her to him.

'Thank you,' he said. 'How can I thank you?' He looked down at her, bent and lightly kissed her forehead. 'Thank you for being my mum today. That's been the nicest thing.'

They drove along the seafront to his flat, and Rosemary gratefully accepted his invitation to come in for a cup of tea.

'My feet are killing me,' she said as she sank down on the tangle of bedclothes on Sam's bed. 'Do you realise we were *two-and-a-half hours* in there?'

He ran downstairs to fill the kettle.

'Sam,' she said thoughtfully, when he returned. 'Were you thinking of bringing your friend home for a cup of tea after the theatre?'

'I don't know. Why?'

He glanced round the room.

'A bit messy, you mean?'

She took a deep breath. This might be the only day she was ever allowed to be his mum. 'Sam, it's filthy. It needs the same treatment you did. It's only a little room. We could clean it up by Friday. We could paint it!'

He shrugged. 'OK. Well, we could clean up a bit. I haven't got any paint.'

So it came about that they spent the rest of the afternoon buying paint and brushes, collecting Rosemary's hoover, bucket and rags, and raiding her airing cupboard for clean sheets and blankets for his bed. ('You mean you *never* wash them?' she gasped incredulously. 'Oh, well, yes,' he replied. 'In the summer sometimes.')

She also collected a couple of cushions from her living room, called up to Maxwell to get himself fish and chips, and they piled into the car again.

'What about your carpet?' She paused at the top of the drive.

'What about it?'

'It's in holes.'

'We could take it to the tip, I guess.'

'Let's take the big Chinese rug from my living room.'

'Oh, no, Rosemary, hang on. . . .'

'No, let's. There's a fitted carpet, perfectly good, underneath. Come on! Help me roll it up!'

Anxiously, protesting, he followed her.

It took them two days of very hard work. Late on Thursday evening they collapsed, exhausted—Rosemary prone on the bed, Sam stretched out on the floor. The room smelled of new paint. They had painted it white, and Rosemary had brought a table lamp, and a bright patchwork blanket to cover the bed. Her Chinese rug all but covered the floor. Everywhere was clean, orderly, beautiful, transformed from squalor to cosy simplicity. Rosemary had even managed to fit Sam's belongings inside the cupboard, and brought a bedside locker from home for his clothes. They had picked up a small bookcase, to house his piles of books, from a second-hand shop which they had passed on the way back from the tip. ('Sam, look!' Rosemary had exclaimed, excited. 'That bookcase would just fit under your window.'

'Oh, no, Rosemary. No more money. You've spent too much; I can't—'

'Don't be silly! Come on!' And she was right. It did just fit under the window.)

'You can put your new clothes on now,' she said, in weary contentment, 'and it's only Thursday.'

Apprehension fluttered unpleasantly in Sam's belly at the thought of Friday.

'She might not like me,' he said. It was not so hard to say it looking up at the calm, remote whiteness of the sloping ceiling, lit by the warm glow of the lamp. Easier than looking at someone's face to say it—even Rosemary's.

'More fool her if she doesn't.'

'I've tried saying things like that to myself, but it doesn't work. I'm so scared she won't want me. She's so beautiful, Rosemary. I almost wish she'd said "no". It would be easier than waiting for her not to like me; not to want me.'

He fell silent a moment, and Rosemary tried in vain to think of something encouraging to say. Sam lay looking up at the ceiling. Softly, shy to say it, but unable to keep to himself any longer the yearning inside him—the helpless, overflowing passion of yearning—he said:

'Had I no eyes, but ears, my ears would love
That inward beauty and invisible:
Or, were I blind, thy outward parts would move
Each part in me that were but sensible:
Though neither eyes nor ears, to hear nor see,
Yet should I be in love, by touching thee.'

He groaned and rolled over onto his belly, rubbing his face restlessly in the crook of his arm.

'Dear me,' said Rosemary, 'you *are* far gone.'

They did not speak for a while, silent each in their own thoughts. Then Rosemary asked him, 'Sam; tell me to mind my own business if you like, and I'm not telling you what to do, but why don't you look for a job?'

He rolled onto his back again and lay gazing up at the ceiling again.

'I have a job,' he said, 'or at least an occupation. Well, a social function. Sam Rowley, pariah.'

Rosemary sat up and looked at him severely.

'Can't you promote yourself? Sam Rowley, wage-earner would be an improvement.'

'Rosemary—' he hesitated. 'You've been a good mum to me these last few days. Would you mind very much if you stop now? Just be my friend again.'

He moved his head and glanced across at her.

'I'm sorry—' they both said at once. Rosemary laughed.

'I wasn't meaning to criticise you. Truly I just wondered why.'

Sam sat up and hugged his arms round his knees. He spoke abruptly.

'I had a breakdown when I was seventeen, then another and another. I couldn't hack it, couldn't do the stuff—you know, offices, desks, paper, college courses. They ran me at all kinds of hurdles, and I couldn't make it over any of them. I'd get up in the morning and it was a wall of nightmare, the day looming up at me. My family even sent me to art school, that being the most Bohemian and frivolous activity they could think of. Art, sadly, is a tight and demanding discipline, requiring fanatical dedication and considerable talent. I got out of the whole scene before they could decide to try me on ballet.

'I'd had it, anyway, with their ECT and their pills and their analysis; shrinks with eyes like revolving dinner plates spreading my guts on the table with their long dry fingers, picking through my torn-up, freaked-out head for a grain of conformity. I was even less employable after all of that. It rattles your head a bit, all the treatment . . . affects you. Co-ordination and memory . . . um . . . and so on. . . .' His voice trailed away vaguely, and he put out a hand and stroked his fingertips gently along the raised pattern of leaves on the rug.

'I do a bit of work, here and there. Hop-picking in the summer sometimes. I used to pick up work on the building sites, but times are bad. You can't get work like that so easily now. You have to know the right people. You know how it is. Well, maybe you don't.'

'No,' said Rosemary in a small voice. 'I don't think I have the faintest idea how it is. But I'm beginning to understand why tomorrow is so scary and so important. Sam, I'll pray for you.'

He smiled. 'Pray for me? Will you? I'd like that. I've prayed, sometimes. Midnight prayers, you know, "Get me out of this!" That kind of thing. And once with a rubber clamp in my teeth on the treatment table, with tears running down my face, "I hate you, God." I don't think I'll ever make a saint.'

Rosemary swallowed. 'Sam, would you pray with me now?'

Her hands were clenched tight and she stared down at her knees. She didn't dare look at him, though she could feel him looking at her. This was either what he needed or else it was the worst thing of all to say. Rosemary couldn't tell which.

'All right,' he said.

'OK. Let us pray,' Rosemary squeaked, before either of them had time to think better of it, and she bowed her head.

All the prayers Rosemary had ever heard had been very polite to God, and mindful of his exalted status. She could recall none with the urgency and directness she needed just now. 'Thou leadest me beside still waters' was simply not in it. She needed to grab God by the arms and shake him hard and shout, *'Move it, will you!'* in his face.

'Heavenly Father,' she began. 'Heavenly Father . . . heavenly Father . . . Sam, I just don't know what to say.'

Sam shifted onto his knees, and knelt with his hands clasped and his head bent, his hair falling forward, obscuring his face.

'God, if you're there, please help me. Please. I'm sorry I said I hate you. But I did hate you. I did hate you then. It felt like you'd got something against me. Oh God, if you love me . . . if you love me . . . please, oh please . . . Eleanor. Let me hold her in my arms and kiss her. Even just once.'

There was in his voice, quiet and simple, the opened out agony of his soul.

Rosemary had once seen a televised surgical operation on someone's back, in which she watched the surgeon peel back skin and muscle and flesh until the very bones of the prone patient were laid bare. Watching that was a bit like listening to Sam's prayer. She wished she had never suggested it.

'Amen,' she muttered, feebly.

She realised that she would spend every waking minute of the next twenty-four hours praying with everything in her this prayer. She had little hope of it being the sort of thing you could ask God. Maxwell said that to ask God to do anything was a naive and primitive form of magic; that Christian prayer was a submission to the purposes of God—'Thy will be done.'

Rosemary thought he was probably right. She thought maybe it was permissible to pray for people to accept their miseries—for the victims of volcanoes to be comforted and the sick to be at peace. But this prayer of Sam's . . . the problem with it was that it would be possible to tell whether or not it had been answered.

Maxwell said that the prayer 'Thy will be done' was the

highest, hardest endeavour. But it wasn't. Or maybe it was for Jesus, who knew what God's will was, but for Maxwell and Rosemary and Sam, who hadn't the faintest idea what God wanted them to do, there was far more risk in the prayer that said, 'Oh God, if you love me . . . Eleanor,' than in the vague acquiescence of: 'Thy will be done.'

With a mixture of resentment, excitement, awe, Rosemary realised that she was bound up with Sam in this. Somehow she had joined him in the place where his spirit stood, face raised to the answerless dark, calling out to the silent God he so wanted to be there. It occurred to her that if a hollow and distant voice boomed back at him, '*My* will be done,' that might not be a God Sam had much use for. The prayer had been an opening of his soul to God. If God's response came to no more than, 'It's my ball and I'm going home,' Rosemary felt she would then be in a difficult position, because she didn't want that kind of God either. She didn't want Maxwell's God who had to have his own way all the time. She didn't want a God who was always out.

Trust in God, Maxwell said, was what the Christian faith was all about. Yes, all right, but a God who sometimes did something. Not a God indefinitely absent in heaven while Sam broke his heart here on earth. The Sunday God was no good for this, nor the sophisticated God endlessly out-smarting his children and sending them away empty-handed. The God within was no use either: perpetual source of treacly serenity doling out platitudes for dead-end situations. It was all right to trust God, but let that be a solid bulwark of a God; not a ghostly, absent God. They needed a God of uncompromising otherness and pre-sence—the God who is *there*.

Sam knelt still. He stretched out his hands, held open in supplication.

'Be there for me,' he whispered. 'Be there for me. I know I've done a bum deal on you, but I can't offer you bribes and brittle promises—I'll be no better tomorrow. Because of your lovingkindness, be there for me. Please. Just once.'

And if I were God, Rosemary reflected, I'd rather have this young man making me no promises, throwing himself on my mercy, than all the bowing and scraping congregations offering me the worship I require, on condition that I mind my own business and don't try to get mixed up with their lives.

As she drove home that night, as she lay in bed and waited for sleep to come, as her eyes opened the next morning, and through all the tasks of the day, Rosemary's soul beat on God's door and begged: 'Oh God, God who is there; if you love him, if you love him; let him hold Eleanor in his arms and kiss her. But give him something real, oh God. Not just once.'

Friday evening the wind blew cold and dismal along the seafront, the sky clumped in clouds of sullen purple and steely grey. The sea-road was as busy with cars as ever, but there were few people about on foot. The long battered terrace of tall buildings; boarding houses, cheap hotels, holiday flats, a huddle of shops, offered their closed and weathered faces, gallery of the dead, in mute endurance of the sea wind.

The barking cry of the news-vendor, 'Evening Press! Evening Press!' lost itself among the shrieks of the wheeling seagulls. It was not raining, but it might as well have been.

Twenty-five to seven Sam stood by the railings near the newspaper kiosk, looking out across the heaving sea. He knew he would have been even earlier if he had not spent the afternoon at Rosemary's house, bathing, washing his hair. ('*Blow-dry* it? Hair-dryers are for ladies!')

'Don't be silly, Sam. Sit still and let me get the tangles out.'

'Ouch! What? No, I don't want you to trim my beard.')

He had been glad of her company alleviating his jitters, and then glad of the walk from her house; of the bracing and unsympathetic wind.

The spray blew like fine rain, and his hair whipped damp and salty across his face. He turned and leaned back on the railings. He stood very still. It was the only way to hold steady in the turmoil of hope and fear and pleading and anxiety. Rosemary had offered him a meal after he had bathed, but he had refused it. His stomach had balled up in desperate spasm. Hope and terror were running amok in his guts, his head, his knees.

Walking through the town centre to the seafront, at five to seven, Eleanor was also afraid. She had not seen Sam since Tuesday. The momentary, magic inspiration of crazy courage, in which she had accepted his invitation, began to look more like folly the more she reflected on it.

Everything in her upbringing, everything in her common sense, told her that only a girl of the most awesome and dangerous stupidity would go alone on a date with a man of whom she knew nothing except that he was unkempt, out of work and took drugs.

Her footsteps slowed, and she almost changed her mind and went home. As she hesitated, thinking carefully, she reminded herself that that was not quite all she knew. Those were the outside things. Looking very hard into his eyes across the snack bar counter she had seen integrity, and the hard gem of humility which remains when illusions and pretension have been burned away. Then there had been that shining loveliness of joy about him when she said 'yes'. It would be coldest cruelty to puncture that shining gift of joy. Besides all that, she did very much want to see *Twelfth Night*. She let her misgivings slip through her fingers to the wind, and carried on walking.

She saw Sam in the distance, as the road took her onto the seafront, hunched against the cold, his hair blowing back in the wind. He was looking up at the clock. And now he had seen her too, turned to face her, was walking slowly towards her. It reminded her of two cowboys in a gun battle in a late-night Saturday Western. She saw herself walking along, and she thought, 'Ellie, you shouldn't be doing this.' And then they stood face to face.

A hundred things Sam had practised saying. He forgot them all. The wind blew his hair across his face, and he brushed it away with his hand.

'You came. I didn't think you'd come,' he said.

There was tension in his face, a shadow. Anxiety had suffocated joy. Too badly he wanted it to be all right. She had come, and that was what he wanted, but he felt powerless to make it work out right. He needed her reassurance that she had come because she wanted to come, not just because she had promised.

'Of course I came,' she said. 'I've been looking forward to it.'

She saw the springing of hope, of happiness again in his eyes. She reached out, and with her fingertips lightly touched his hand. 'I have,' she said.

He stood looking down at her still, and smiled suddenly, relaxing. The wind blew about them. Sam was used to the cold, but Eleanor shivered.

'Let's go inside,' she said. 'It's freezing.'

The foyer of the elderly theatre, brightly lit in its brave and faded elegance, hummed with people. As the bell rang for the start of the performance, and they moved towards the doors of the stalls, the pressing crowd jostled them together. Sam laid his hand gently on her shoulder. She looked up at him, excited, happy, and he smiled at her, the joy dancing in his eyes again. It was all right. It was all right. It was all right.

'F26,' he said.

'What?'

'Row F. Seats 26 and 27. Should be aisle seats.'

His hand lingered on her arm, guiding her into the row.

His touch was light, respectful, and made no claims; did not invade her, or attempt to assert intimacy.

It was an enchanted moment, sitting together in the shabby velvet and gold of the theatre, as the lights dimmed and the curtain rose on the Illyrian palace—'*If music be the food of love, play on . . .*'—and they were drawn into the world of elegant phrase and courtly gesture, delighted again by the wit and energy of Shakespeare's verse. Even the critics in their world-weary scepticism, lounging arrogantly in complimentary seats, had to admit it was a good production; but for Sam and Eleanor, it was spell-binding, and that was because they saw it together.

Afterwards, they walked down the steps of the theatre, out into the darkness. Neither of them spoke, caught up still in the enchantment of the play. They wandered over the wide pavement to the crossing, not touching each other, but encircled in one communion. The pedestrian light stood at red, and the road was still busy with cars even though it was late. They stood waiting for the lights to change. Sam looked down at her.

'"*Good madam, let me see your face.*"'

She smiled up at him. '"*Have you any commission from your lord to negotiate with my face? You are now out of your text*"—oh, the light's green!'

They crossed the road and strolled along the promenade to the railings, leaned over them and looked down at the pounding sea, reflecting and distorting the lights of the town.

After a while Eleanor said, 'Shall we go somewhere and get a cup of coffee?'

For a moment Sam said nothing, then: '"*By your patience, no. My stars shine darkly over me: the malignancy of my fate might, perhaps, distemper yours; therefore, I shall crave of you your leave, that I may bear my evils alone. It were a bad recompense for your love, to lay any of them on you.*" Actually, I haven't got any money. I was going to ask you if you'd like to come and have a cup of tea with me at my flat, 'cause it's only just down the road, but I thought hardly knowing me you'd probably say "no".'

Eleanor thought carefully. This was a delicate situation. '". . . *being prompted by your present trouble, out of my lean and low ability I'll lend you something: my having is not much; I'll make division of my present with you: Hold, there's half my coffer."* '

Sam laughed. 'You know the play as well as I do. *"Madam, I am most apt to embrace your offer."* Let's stand here a minute, and watch the sea. As you like: we can go back to my place or you can buy us a coffee. I don't mind.'

'If I ask you a question, will you tell me the truth?'

'*"What shall you ask of me that I'll deny?"*'

'No, seriously, Sam. Tell me honestly. I'd like to talk to you. I feel as though I know you, but I don't know you. But if we go to a café, and I pay, will that embarrass you? We can go to your flat, if you'd rather.'

'*"Go with me to my house, and hear thou there how many fruitless pranks this ruffian hath botch'd up, that thou thereby mays't smile . . ."* Yes, I am embarrassed. Yes, I'd feel more comfortable at my place. But I would well understand you feeling wary.'

'Perhaps I should. I don't though. OK, let's go to your place. Let's go now. It's cold.'

They walked along the seafront, not speaking, but very aware of each other. For Eleanor, the people at the snack bar had been as remote and separate as people on television or in a play; the other side of the counter, dwellers of a world she did not understand and vaguely dreaded—a grim and threatening world of prison and homelessness and drugs. Minds fuddled and personalities made unpredictable by alcohol and mental illness, she was concerned for them, but it meant a lot to have the counter between them and herself.

Now here was Sam, as surprising as an actor stepped off

the stage and come to talk to her, as hard to come to terms with as a real person materialising on her hearth rug out of the television. And she liked him. She liked him very much. She was as alert as she could be for signs of danger, but all she could sense in him were things she had never connected with the people of the snack bar: gentleness, intelligence, education, respect.

She glanced up at him as he walked beside her, his hair and his beard blowing in the wind.

'You look like Jesus, walking by the sea,' she said.

'Me?' He laughed. 'The resemblance starts and finishes on the outside. He spent his life putting things right, I've spent mine messing them up. He achieved what he set out to do. Me . . . I can't even begin.'

'Jesus was crucified.' Having said that, Eleanor felt suddenly anxious in case it sounded preachy and trite. He glanced down at her, and then away again.

'Yes,' he said. 'Well, that I can identify with.'

'I think,' Eleanor replied cautiously, 'I don't want to sound sanctimonious, um, vicar's daughter and all that, but I think that was why he let it happen.'

'You're a vicar's daughter?'

'Yes.'

'This is where my flat is. Don't know why I call it a flat. It's a bedsit really. Top floor. Are you feeling strong?'

She followed him up the flights of stairs, he pressing in the time switch for the light on each floor. At the top, he opened the door of his room and stood aside for her to go in.

'Don't you keep your door locked? Oh, Sam, what a lovely room!' she exclaimed as he switched on the lamp. 'Oh, it must be beautiful in the day to look out across the sea.'

Sam smiled. 'I suppose so. I've got used to it. Most often I lie on my back and look at the ceiling. Make yourself at home. I'll go and fill the kettle.'

Eleanor sat on the bed, and looked at his room in its orderly simplicity.

'Thank you, Rosemary. Oh thank you, Rosemary,' Sam was whispering in his heart as he filled the kettle and climbed the stairs again.

'Your room smells of new paint,' Eleanor remarked, as Sam knelt and plugged in the kettle. 'It's a nice, clean smell. Come to think of it, you're looking very respectable this evening. Have you come into some money?

'I'm sorry,' she added hastily. 'I feel as though I know you better than I do. That was a rude thing to say, wasn't it?'

He looked over his shoulder at her, laughing.

'No,' he said, shuffling across the floor on his knees to root in the cupboard for the tea. 'And no I haven't come into any money, but . . . I can't find a thing in this cupboard now Rosemary's tidied it up—oh, here it is.'

'Who's Rosemary?'

Sam had said it without thinking. The disappointment and suspicion in Eleanor's voice gave him a feeling in his gut like riding a roller coaster. She cares, he thought, the incredulous hope of it momentarily tightening his throat, stopping his breath. She doesn't want there to be anyone else.

'Rosemary,' he said, putting a teabag into the teapot Rosemary had given him (after severely pointing out to him that it was a waste of money to use a teabag for each person), 'is my fairy godmother.'

The kettle boiled and he poured the water into the pot.

'That's why I sounded surprised about you being a vicar's daughter. Rosemary is a vicar's wife. Or at least, I don't think they call them vicars in her church.'

'Oh, maybe I know her! What's her surname?' Sam heard the lightness and relief in her voice at Rosemary's married status. Happiness fluttered inside him.

'Yes, you probably do know her. Her surname's Harrison.'

'Harrison? Rosemary Harrison? Maxwell Harrison's wife? That was the one who disappeared, wasn't it? How did you come to know her?'

Sam poured the tea and handed her a mug.

'I met her while she was being invisible. We stayed friends. She spends Sunday afternoons with me and my friends.'

Me and my friends. Eleanor felt a sudden stab of jealousy at that, of wanting to be included. Who were his friends?

'That sounds nice,' she said.

Sam was familiar with the feeling of being shut out. He recognised it in someone else.

'Why don't you come up on Sunday?' he said.

Her ready acceptance of this invitation started up a long forgotten song of gladness in him. He was going to see her again. Something was going right. Something was working out. Inevitably, he felt terror mix with the joy. In his experience, the higher the hope, the harder he hit when he crashed.

'Why did you say Rosemary is your fairy godmother?' Eleanor asked.

'You would too, if you'd seen my room before she got to work on it on Tuesday. She bought me these clothes as well. And I only asked if I could use her bath.'

Eleanor's question hung unspoken in the air, and Sam knew what she was asking.

'She knew how important this evening was to me,' he said.

This, he knew, was not a good romantic tactic. 'Treat 'em mean, keep 'em keen,' Alessandro said, and that worked remarkably well for him; but Sam did not want that. If Sam being vulnerable, and desperately wanting her, bored Eleanor, then she was in for a lot of boredom and she'd better know it now.

'Oh.' A fragile moment hung between them, as Eleanor

cautiously examined the implications of this. Sam couldn't bear it. He looked through his stack of records, found a Mozart concerto, put it on the record player. Music to draw over the emotional weight of silence.

'It's all right if I put a record on?' He paused, and asked the question as he held the arm ready to put in place on the record. She smiled at him, mischievous, knowing he was running for cover, had let her see too much of his heart.

'"*If music be the food of love*,"' she said, '"*play on*."'

For a few minutes, music alone filled the room with its precise joy, the disciplined, winging freedom of its beauty. The two of them sat together, quiet. Eleanor drank her tea, watched Sam close his eyes, the music alive in his hands, in his face—movement under stillness. Then as she sat watching him, he opened his eyes, and he was looking straight into her eyes, the stream of his soul fused with hers, unguarded, momentous. Five minutes, a second, a lifetime? It was a brief eternal space, his being opening to hers, and hers to his; a recognition something akin to a promise. Then he ducked his head out of it, and drank his tea.

Into the silence that sparkled electric between them, they both spoke at once, and looked at each other and laughed.

'I don't know anything about you,' said Sam. 'Nothing except that you fry a slice of bread well and you have trouble with sums.'

'What shall I tell you?'

'Anything. Do you believe in fairies? Have you seen the exhibition of photographs in the Woolton Street Gallery? Do you write your name in the sand by the sea?'

And she had so much to tell him, because he wasn't especially interested that she was a Sociology student, but he understood about the way she could smell the dawn rising, and how the ominous mooing of the fog warning made her afraid in the night.

She told him about the day in the summer she had swum

in the sea when it was really too rough, wanting to join in the joyous play of the white horses and ride on the waves. Then getting out, the surf had flung her to the ground, rolled her cruelly on the sliding shingle, pelted her with pebbles, and she had felt childishly upset all week that the sea she had loved as a friend could push her over and throw stones at her.

She told him about the afternoon last autumn when, walking home to her digs after lectures, she had heard a tiny sound in the hedge, and looking towards it had been entranced by the sight of a mouse, unaware of her, sitting up in the banked grass and plant debris, eating a leaf.

'And you?' she said. 'What about you?'

And he had to admit to her the abysmal, gnawing loneliness, and wanting to get back on his feet again, and being always so damned afraid.

It was late when he walked home with her ('I'll be all right alone.' 'Eleanor, it's after midnight.' 'I'll be OK.' 'Please. Please let me come with you . . . I don't want to say goodbye.' 'That's different then; that's OK') along the sea's edge, then up through the town. Eleanor felt embarrassed by the relative opulence of her home. St Peter's Vicarage: detached, its own drive, well-to-do neighbourhood—a long walk from Sam's place.

The house was all in darkness but for the light inside in the hallway, which her parents had left on for her.

As they reached the front door, she turned to say goodnight. She couldn't see his face, because of the street light shining in the road behind him, but she felt his stillness, his not wanting to leave her, his soul beseeching hers not to let it end. He didn't move though; didn't speak. He was giving the freedom of the moment to her as a gift, letting her make of their parting what she would.

Some small, hard-headed part of Eleanor put in a final bid for caution: 'There is something wrong with this man. He is not of your kind. He has no job. He has long hair. He smokes (not just tobacco either). He is outside society. This man is a pariah. Be wary. Let it rest here.' She honestly couldn't tell if it was meanness or common sense.

It felt a long time to both of them that she stood hesitating, holding his gift of freedom to take or leave him, which was all he had to offer.

Then she took one step towards him. 'Sam,' she whispered, hesitantly stretching out her hand to him. And she was close in his arms, held close, close against the beating of his heart and the bushy softness of his beard, her head resting against his collar bone (how *thin* he is!), smelling the clean, warm smell of him, the clothes that still smelled of the department store, his hair and his beard that smelled of Maxwell's shampoo.

His hand moved, tender, stroking her hair, and she lifted her face to his, wanting him, seeking his kiss.

A Many Splendoured Thing

*But the man was anxious to justify himself
and said to Jesus, 'And who is my neighbour?' (Luke 10: 29).*

A Many Splendoured Thing

You would not have known, to look at Eric Barton, that he
was a man of strict and passionate convictions. He didn't
look that way at all. He had a mild, pinkish, indeterminate
sort of face, faintly obscured by more or less square steel-
rimmed glasses, and wispily decorated with thinning grey
hair. Plumpish, verging on tubby, and of barely average
height, he clothed himself in lightish coloured hopsack
trousers and any one of various acrylic woollies in harm-
less pastel shades. Underneath the woollies he wore
coloured shirts in vague and discreet hues, short-sleeved
in the summer, and long-sleeved over a vest in the winter.

He was one of three CDT teachers at a comprehensive
school half a mile down the road from his home. Every
morning at seven minutes past eight he left his medium-
sized red-brick semi-detached house, in the quiet and
moderate suburban road where he lived, and walked to
work because the exercise was good for him and because
he liked the fresh air.

It would be an exaggeration to say he actually liked his
job, though the terror he had fought when he stood before
his first class as a student teacher thirty-two years ago,
now had its place in his gallery of memories, no more

than a dusty curiosity. Nowadays he slipped into his working role effortlessly; the days seemed neither short nor long, the students all much the same as each other.

His pupils left his tuition soundly taught but scarcely educated. Imagination was not his strong point.

Sundays and Tuesday evenings, however, revealed the sterner stuff of his spirit. For Eric Barton was a man of fervent and narrow Christian belief, an elder and house-group leader in Mount Grace Baptist Church: a man respected, a man who knew what was right.

On Sunday mornings at five past ten, he and his wife Amy set out in their Fiat Panda, which was getting old but looked like new, for Mount Grace. They would park as near the huge forbidding Victorian church building as they could, and walk peacefully along the pavement towards it, Eric with his Bible tucked under his arm, Amy holding hers in her hands. They would pause and look at this week's crop of posters outside the church ('CRUCIFIED FOR YOU! FIND OUT MORE ON SUNDAY' 'WHAT'S MISSING FROM THIS CH--CH?—U R !'), then mingle convivially with the incoming congregation, Eric stooping to pick up any bits of litter that had blown through the black iron railings into the strip of paving that ran along the front of the church.

Their lodger, Simon Groves, the English Head of Department from Eric's school, they left behind at home on a Sunday morning. To maintain consistency with biblical teaching, the Bartons would not have entertained the idea of housing an unbeliever, but Simon attended the Anglo-Catholic church of Holy Redeemer, where he served at the altar as an acolyte once a month, and led the congregation in their singing of the psalm at eleven o'clock Mass, most Sundays. The fact that Holy Redeemer was an Anglican and not Roman Catholic church brought it within the fold of the kingdom in Eric Barton's understanding, but only by a whisker. He and Amy prayed for their lodger at night before they went to bed.

Not that they had any complaints about Simon. Quiet and cheerful, his bright-eyed, clean-cut presence had a lightness about it that was pleasant about the house. Naturally unobtrusive, they could forget he was there at times, until he popped his head round the sitting room door of an evening: 'Anyone else for coffee?'

Most weeks he would invite David, the verger from his church, round for a glass of beer on one or two evenings, but that seemed to be the extent of his social life. Sometimes he and David went on walking weekends across the Downs together, and Eric enjoyed those times when he and Amy had the house to themselves. Nevertheless, he was pleased to see Simon home again when they came in from evening service on Sunday. Eric and Amy had no children of their own, and they liked having Simon about the place. He felt almost like family.

'You should come along to the Mount Grace family fun night, Simon,' Amy would say to him. 'You're nearly thirty. It's time you got married and settled down, found a place of your own. I bet there's hardly any young people at Holy Redeemer—and besides, you don't get to know people by sharing a hymnbook! You should come along to Mount Grace and meet some of the ladies.'

She spoke with coquettish humour, but she meant it. She and Eric had been house-group leaders for a long time. They had a very clear understanding of how people were made, and what their needs were. Amy particularly was respected in the church for her counselling skills. She had got Richard Andrews' new wife Alice making coffee at the toddler group, and was working gently but with determination on the dismantling of Alice's dangerously feminist inclinations.

It was Amy's firm persistence that had got Jean Kirkwood driving, and look, Jean had passed her test in May. It was usually poor Amy who fielded Jerry Saunders after service when he had one of his depressions. She took a very positive line with him; reminded him of all his blessings; told him to stop dwelling on the problems of life; told him he mustn't feel guilty about his mother's death, he had nothing with which to reproach himself, and that was all behind him now.

It was Amy whom Susan Smith confided in about her eating problem—the need to consume Mars Bars, biscuits, anything. And Amy had tactfully explained to her that a Tupperware box of peeled and quartered carrots kept in the fridge made a nice alternative snack.

Amy had done the advanced counselling course, and helped at the Pregnancy Crisis Centre on Wednesday mornings. She led the team of counsellors who ministered on a Sunday evening. People went out from her presence both chastened and inspired by Amy's positive and self-disciplined approach to life. Slim, well-groomed and smiling, she was the image of Christian womanhood. And sometimes, privately, she would shake her head sadly over the stubbornness of some of the church members' problems: they never seemed to progress to standing on their own two feet in spite of all her advice and prayer.

With Simon, she got exactly nowhere. He would laugh good-humouredly at her attempts to encourage him into the social circles of Mount Grace, but had the knack of evading the net with courteous skill. She had tried for a long time to persuade him to come and join them at their Tuesday night house-group meeting, but then he had enrolled for fitness classes at the Sports Centre, which unfortunately took place on a Tuesday evening.

At the moment, this house group was embarking on the study of St Paul's letters to the Corinthians, as part of a programme of study on the character of a Christian which presently formed the theme of teaching on Sunday evenings at Mount Grace. Eric had spoken last Tuesday at house group on the end of the first chapter of First Corinthians, about how God liked to choose those people who were low and despised in the sight of others, and would use those whom the strong and self-righteous thought nothing of, to shame them in their self-satisfaction and teach them a better wisdom than their blinkered vision had allowed. Exegesis was Eric's skill (pastoral ministry he left to Amy, especially the tearful variety) and he expounded the passage well.

As he talked, he balanced his Bible comfortably in his hand, well-thumbed and familiar, the manual of the Christian life, the route-map of the narrow path of the righteous through the treacherous landscape of sin and disaster that contoured society round about.

The Barton household followed an orderly and steady routine, week by week. Church on Sunday, house group on Tuesday. Once a month Amy and Eric went out to an inexpensive restaurant for dinner. On Saturdays they shopped in the supermarket and had coffee and a cream bun in a café afterwards. Indeed, in some buried, un-acknowledged corner of his being, it was that cream bun that was the highlight of Eric's week. Amy viewed his sweet tooth with some severity, and the Saturday cream bun represented a joyous release from discipline.

Other than that, and Simon's weekends away, the round of days was shaped by routine chores: washing up, cleaning teeth, vacuuming the carpet. Amy worked as a home help three mornings a week, and the rest of her time she dedicated to dusting and polishing her house, and solving other people's problems.

In the evening, they watched the six o'clock news. After that Eric might have school work to do, and Simon would disappear to his room, or go out to the pub with David. The Bartons did not feel entirely easy about his going to the pub, nor about some of the television programmes he liked to watch, but they were broad-minded enough to live with it.

This uneventful routine might have stretched on indefinitely, had not Eric arrived home from school one afternoon to find on the kitchen table a tear-stained note from Amy to say she had left. She was in love, the note said, and mentioned a man from Mount Grace (also married). They just couldn't go on living a lie. They were going to live at his holiday cottage in Bournemouth. She had taken most of her things, and would come back for the rest during the week, while Eric was at school. She didn't want to see him, or discuss it. She wanted a clean break. She signed off with her love.

Eric sank down onto a kitchen chair, holding the note in his hand, staring at it in disbelief. He read it a second time. He sat there a long while, just looking at it, stunned. For him, home was home and school was school. When he left home in the morning, the mantle of the day gradually settled upon him, so that by the time he had walked the half-mile to school, home and Amy no longer existed for him. It had never occurred to him to wonder what housewives did during the day.

Eric's soul had no tools for dealing with a situation like this. They had always worked together, he and Amy; and this was Amy's department: tears, domestic trauma, relationships in crisis, trembling people with haunted eyes. These ragged and ghastly untidinesses did not intimidate her in the slightest. How many times had he watched her weighing up the prospect of people whose lives were scattered about them in disorderly bits; fragile lives that had been played with too roughly and all come apart? Amy, with her lips set in a firm line, and the same look in her eyes as a woman purposefully rolling her sleeves up, to confront the disgraceful mess.

He needed her now to defy his own mess, his own disgrace, and his mind refused the concept that Amy had made this mess. It must be his mess. Amy's life was so orderly, so full of solutions. Locked inside her neat and presentable head she had the enviable answer-book to the tough and incomprehensible problems that defeated everyone else. And she had taken it away, leaving him by himself with this letter. This letter, and a domestic routine that was too small and ordinary to accommodate a crisis of grief and shame.

Eric felt as though something appallingly, stupidly inappropriate had happened, like being bequeathed an elephant, and having it looking in at him through the kitchen window; an elephant of vast appetite, uncertain habits and horribly evident strength; someone else's unwanted, surplus, unwelcome elephant. This situation was too big for him. It belonged to someone else.

Eric's soul contracted. Like a viewer watching television unaware that the final programme was ending, unaware of the significance of the National Anthem playing, watching the comfortable, anaesthetic flow of images come to an end, contract to a small white dot, leave him finally alone staring at a blank and empty screen, with hours yet to fill. It was the same feeling as pulling the plug out while he still sat in the bath, watching the water retreating until it had all gone, leaving him cold and damp and heavy, a pointless body in an empty bath, searching for the energy to get out, do something about it, pick up a towel.

Missing Amy was not the issue at that moment. He had been married to her for too long to know if he loved her. She was simply indispensable, part of him. The tide that had gone out was an exemplary lifestyle, an orderly working model of married life. It left him beached there, sitting on the kitchen chair staring at the tear-stained, neatly-written note.

But as the returning tide crept up and touched him, it was a different water, an uncongenial cold sea of disgrace, embarrassment, shame.

The first returning thoughts that seeped into his numb brain taunted him with the prospect of having to tell people. His colleagues at school. The members of his church. The neighbours. His elderly mother. The milkman. The lodger, who would walk through the door any moment now. How did one say such a thing? Gravely, as one mentioned the victims of famine and flood in Sunday morning intercessions? Soberly, as one shared the news of someone else's bereavement? In shocked disapproval, as one spoke of homosexual marriages? Casually, so as not to breathe the sour contamination of one's own losses into someone else's face? There was no way to say something that should not be said at all; to speak the lines scripted for somebody else, that did not belong to the role he had always played.

For the moment, the searing embarrassment of disgrace obliterated everything else. Life had come to a stop. Love and sorrow were trivial, irrelevant emotions compared with the shame of having the whole façade crumble around him; the hateful, sickening nakedness of being no better than anyone else. Curious eyes would look at him, seeing how an elder of the church looks when his wife makes a fool of him and leaves him in the lurch. Someone would suggest he go for counselling. Everyone would pray for him, as he and Amy had prayed for Simon in their quiet time last thing at night. Prayers of the faithful that looked down from their high pier of righteousness on failed lives struggling helplessly in the ooze and sludge below.

At times like this, other men—men in books and films—swore and lit a cigarette, found refuge in a bottle of whisky while they thought what to do next. But Eric didn't smoke or drink or swear, because he was a Baptist elder; he wasn't the sort of man whose wife left him, so he didn't need that kind of thing. He hadn't got any whisky or cigarettes, and swearing was dirty.

Then, suddenly, Simon was in the kitchen.

'Hullo. Had a good day? Have you had a cup of tea? Amy not in? Eric, what's wrong?'

Eric couldn't speak, couldn't voice the shameful, embarrassing thing, didn't look at him, handed him the note in silence. In silence Simon read it. Perhaps that would be it. Perhaps there would be silence for ever now: a grave, shocked silence beholding Amy's adultery and the humiliation of Eric's insufficiency.

'Oh, God,' said Simon. 'When did you get this?'

'Just now. It was on the kitchen table when I came in.'

'Ouch.'

He read the note again. He looked at Eric as he handed it back to him. The look in his eyes recognised and understood the situation, made no judgements, was a massive relief. For one moment Eric was overwhelmingly glad that Simon would not offer to pray with him, would not offer him the sterile consolation of a biblical text. Eric gripped onto the uncondemning recognition of that look. Then Simon turned and picked up the kettle.

'Shall we have a cup of tea?'

We. Life still held a possibility of 'we' then. Simon was choosing to be his ally, not frightened off by the disorder of shame and desertion. He was putting the kettle on. Usually Amy had the kettle on for them. But it was possible to put the kettle on without Amy. For Simon, at any rate.

During the days that followed, the sense persisted in Eric's mind that this was all a dream from which he must awake at any moment; something to laugh at in the sheer relief of consciousness and morning. At school, it was hard to concentrate. He made stupid mistakes, and caught people looking at him oddly; saw the suppressed smirks that told him he'd done something foolish, but he never knew what. Sometimes his eyes would fill with tears, and he would have to stop speaking, stare very hard at any fixed object, fill his mind with nothing—nursery rhymes, multiplication tables, anything—to stem the welling up of pain that wanted to overflow, but must not, must not, must not.

He couldn't eat. Simon took over the cooking, and in the evening would coax him gently to chew his way through a small portion. He couldn't sleep. He lay in bed in the dark, waiting for the respite of oblivion, and it mocked him, withdrew from him, wouldn't come. He would eventually doze fitfully through anxious dreams, and crawl out of bed in the morning to confront the sagging, middle-aged, pointless face that stared dolefully back at him out of the bathroom mirror.

'Eric, I think you should go and see the doctor.'

By the time Simon said that to him, Eric could no more have figured out how to arrange an appointment with the doctor than fly to the moon. The time-worn routine of every day he could trudge through blind, habit taking him through the lessons he'd taught for thirty-two years, and the morning routines of washing, dressing, fastening his tie, and his shoes. Sometimes he forgot an elementary thing—didn't brush his hair, forgot to shave. Simon watched over him, made him eat his breakfast, saw to it that he got to school in one piece.

Apart from that, he continued to host his house group. Simon gave up his fitness classes for the time being, looked after the coffee and biscuits for house group, sat in on the meetings. The first Tuesday after Amy had gone, it had been Simon sitting across the room from him, the look in his eyes throwing a trustworthy rope for Eric to hang on to, that had got him through the shame of breaking the news. Simon never said anything at house group, but it made a difference, having him there.

But the effort of maintaining some shell of appearances at school, church and house group took all Eric's strength.

'I think you should go and see your doctor.'

Eric just shook his head. 'I'll be all right.' Just keeping

going took everything. He had no mind left to use the telephone, fix up a date, drive to the surgery.

'Eric, I can take you.'

Gentleness, understanding. It brought the hateful tears to Eric's eyes. Stare at something, stare. He gritted his teeth till they hurt. Couldn't say thank you. He just nodded.

Simon took him to the doctor. Simon picked up his prescription: pills to make him sleep, pills to dull the pain. Pain? The pain *was* dullness, emptiness, absence. Pills then to dull the dullness, void the emptiness, take away the absence. Eric, like a naked sleepwalker in cold, dense fog, wandered aimlessly in the horror of double vacuum. He discovered that drugged unconsciousness does not deserve the name of sleep. Getting through the day without threat of tears is no relief when the fear has been traded in for a hollow eternal chasm yawning below, around, inside, an echoless, dead silence of the soul—a living death without the lovely austerity of winter or the dear hope of spring.

'I know,' Simon said to him one day. 'It feels like being a shattered windscreen; in place and holding together, but totally, terminally broken. Oh, I know.'

That didn't mean very much to Eric. The words of other people were as meaningless as dismantled machinery, grey pieces of vocabulary that brought no comfort or interest, no communication.

He could sleep at night again, with the medication, and he began to eat again, seeking comfort in bars of chocolate and packets of biscuits, creamy cakes and sticky buns. He ate them with a small, childish, ashamed stubbornness, defying the memory of Amy's disciplined choices. But they didn't touch the empty, aching misery. It just gnawed away more and more of him, until he felt as though there was nothing left.

One afternoon, he came in from school and, without thought or prior planning, left his briefcase in the hall, walking like a dreamer up to the bathroom. He opened the medicine cabinet and took out everything: painkillers (three sorts), vitamins, iron pills, Amy's old sleeping pills, a bottle of tranquillisers dated 1976, pills to dry up catarrh, pills to help fibrositis, four of the pills from his own prescription (Simon had the rest of the bottle in his care).

He held the front of his jumper as a pouch to gather all the bottles in, and he carried them downstairs. He sat down at the kitchen table, and lined them all up in front of him, gazing at them, blankly.

Randomly, without thought or emotion, he began to open the bottles, tipping out the contents of each one, dropping the bottles and lids on the table. He picked up a handful of pills and looked at them: strange, round, interesting little things; long ones, coloured ones; kind, inviting poisons to bring everything to a close. Life that had got too heavy, the round of days that had become an insupportable burden, the bleeding, aching, tearless weariness: to put it all down, and go finally, for ever to sleep. To forget the ache of memories and the confusion of forgetting. That was what he wanted; yes it was. Take them then.

Inside him a small worm of cowardice writhed away from choosing finality. What would God, the God he had lost hope in, but continued to worship on Sunday; the God he could no longer pray to, but whose word he continued to teach at house group—what would that God do to him? What if he fell out of this horror of endless days into the final pit of negation, the seat and root of frozen loneliness, the silent scream of the damned?

Eric threw the handful of pills across the table. He scrabbled his hands among the pills and bottles, convulsive, not knowing what he was doing. Enough—he'd had enough. He couldn't decide any more. He just wanted someone to help him; someone to make it better; someone to put their finger on the livid red spot of agony that all the poison fog was leaking out of; someone to see and realise just how awful it all was.

He slumped forward over the table, beyond dealing with anything, suspended in a nightmare confusion, unable to think, or act, or begin. The telephone rang, and eventually ceased. The clock on the wall continued its discreet electronic ticking. Dust fell into silence—the pitiless silence that had opened like a hole in the world to drag all memory of peace down into despair.

As he sat sprawling across the kitchen table, Eric heard a key turning in the front door lock, along the passage. Simon was home. Amy had always entered brightly with her call of, 'Coo-ee, I'm home!', but Simon padded silently along the passage in his quiet shoes. As he did this evening.

He stood in the kitchen doorway, and took in the sight of Eric in a state of complete collapse, the emptied out pills spilled across the table, the bottles scattered randomly beside them.

Simon put down his raincoat and briefcase, and walked across the kitchen to stand at Eric's side. He put his hand out and touched his shoulder. Simon's touch was not timid or nervous. His hand moulded around Eric's shoulder with a firm, warm pressure. His touch gainsaid the grey, clinging deadness. It asserted a reality of comfort and strength.

'Have you taken any?' he asked. There was no panic in his voice, no horror. He simply sounded as if he cared— not about consequences, but about Eric. And Eric turned, raising his head from the table, hardly looking at Simon, reaching out with shaking, crazy hands for the comfort of Simon's presence. He gripped hold of him, desperately, burrowing his face into Simon's belly, his body racked with dry sobbing. Simon lifted his other hand and gently stroked Eric's head, stood quietly until the wringing agony subsided enough for tears to flow, and Eric's body relaxed into weeping.

'Have you taken any?' he asked again.

Eric shook his head. 'No.' His voice was muffled against Simon's body, and distorted with weeping. 'I was afraid. I. . . .'

A long moan of hopeless misery bled out of him, and his body shuddered in grief.

'That's all right then,' said Simon, tranquilly. This scenario was evidently not foreign to him. He stood quietly, and allowed his body to be used as a refuge and a source of succour for this bankrupt soul, until, after a while, he felt the shaking sobs dying away. Then he gently disengaged himself from Eric's clutching hands. He squatted down beside him, still with his right hand firm and loving on the other man's shoulder, and with the left hand pulled his hanky out of his trouser pocket.

'There,' he said as he wiped away the remains of tears and snot and saliva from Eric's blotched face, as much as had not already soaked into himself. 'There, there. That's better. Now then; how about a cup of tea?'

He stood up, and quickly, without speaking, filled the kettle and switched it on, got out mugs and milk and teapot, and swept the strewn assortment of tablets from the table top into the rubbish bin. He took a chocolate biscuit from the tin on the work surface, unwrapped it and placed it in Eric's hand, poured him a cup of tea, and put it beside him on the table.

Then he pulled out one of the kitchen chairs drawn up to the table, and sat down, composedly sipping his own tea, watching with shrewd compassion as Eric's dazed, stupefied expression gradually resumed normal consciousness after the maelstrom of grief.

Eric reached across the table for his glasses, and settled them on his nose again with a sigh. He looked down at the chocolate biscuit that his hand was holding, and took a bite of it.

'I'm sorry,' he said bleakly, glancing up, self-conscious as returning equilibrium brought embarrassment along with it.

Simon shrugged his shoulders. 'No need to be,' he said. Eric looked down again at the chocolate biscuit in his hand. Amy had fought his weakness for chocolate with unremitting determination for years. He had already eaten three at work. He ought not to be eating this one.

'Amy says it's infantile self-indulgence to respond to life's challenges by eating chocolate,' he said dully.

Simon could have made a comment on Amy's own self-indulgence, compared with which chocolate biscuits seemed fairly innocuous, but he thought better of it.

'I expect she's right,' he said instead. 'So what?'

Yes, so what? She had gone away, with her self-discipline and her determination, and her solutions. And maybe— this new thought appeared like a small, audacious plant on the dead boulders of the moon—maybe there were other ways of doing things, some sort of possibility.

This formed a kind of turning point for Eric. A shivering, feeble hope began to take shape. Life was returning, with its pain and grieving. Sharp, but better than deadness.

Simon stayed in most nights, encouraging Eric to talk, watching television with him, just being there. Sometimes, when he talked, Eric cried. He hated that. It embarrassed him, the feeling of the tears welling up, Simon sitting there seeing his misery. And yet it was that that healed: being seen, someone knowing, not sharing the embarrassment, letting him grieve. The evening he had clung to Simon and wept had been a doorway out of isolation, out of pretending. It had dissolved all the phrases like 'man of the house' and 'big boys don't cry' that had hardened inside him over the years.

Sometimes David, the verger from Simon's church,

would join them for part of the evening, and on one
occasion, when Simon had to be out later than usual on a
school trip, David called round anyway.

Eric felt a little unsure of David. Elegant and tastefully
dressed, with a certain indefinable air of cynicism, he made
Eric feel flabby, passé, dull. It felt comfortable, the three of
them there, but Eric was not sure what he would say to
him without Simon. None the less, he invited him in. It
would not be long before Simon was due home. As the fog
in his mind had cleared, Eric had realised that the two of
them were looking after him, unobtrusively watching over
him, seeing him through. But he could not talk to David in
the way he did to Simon. He would never have let David
see the depths of his unhappiness. He cringed at the
thought of David's sophistication beholding his tears. He
was glad of his company though, and invited him in to the
living room, partly because he had half a suspicion that
Simon might have asked him to call. Simon had seen to it
that he had not been too much alone after the business
with the pills.

Eric felt a sudden surge of gratitude for Simon's thought-
fulness and kindness. He wanted to say it, express it;
wanted David to know that it had not been taken for
granted.

'Thank you—for coming to see me,' he said, glancing shyly at David's face as he sat on the other side of
the room, his legs crossed, draped gracefully in Eric's
armchair. He didn't look like Eric's idea of a verger.

'I do appreciate it, all you've done. You've given up a lot
of time to spend with us here. I mean, you'd probably
rather have been going out to the pub. Thank you.'

David smiled. 'Simon's been worried about you. I told
him you'd be all right, didn't need a nanny, but he
wouldn't have it. "I know what it feels like," he says.
"I'd never forgive myself if he did something awful

because he was alone and it all got too much." He's been counting your every breath, I think.'

'He's been like Jesus to me.' The words blurted out suddenly, an abrupt gout of emotion. 'He has. He's been just like Jesus.'

Running scared from his own strength of feeling, afraid it might start tears again, Eric had to change the subject. David's calmly observant face, with its air of ironical detachment, flustered him, embarrassed him.

'Won't you have some coffee while you're waiting?' he asked. David acquiesced politely to this suggestion, and followed Eric along the passage to the kitchen.

'I don't think Simon thinks of himself as being very God-like,' he said, with a smile in his voice.

'Probably not,' replied Eric, stoutly, 'but it's true what I say. He's been Christ himself to me. We could do with a man like him in our pastoral team at Mount Grace. Indeed we could.'

'Binding up the broken-hearted?'

David stood in the kitchen doorway, leaning against the door frame. 'What I like about Simon,' he said thoughtfully, 'is the kind of skinned air he has. Raw, you know? As though life has skinned him, and he's had the courage to leave it like that, not construct another shell. He looks a bit breathless sometimes, as if he can't quite bear it, but he stays with it. Yes, courage, I suppose that's what I mean. I like his courage. "A man of sorrows, and acquainted with grief." Well, there you go—that's Jesus, isn't it? Maybe that's what you were meaning.'

'He's had difficulties of his own then?' Eric held David's cup of coffee out to him.

'What, Simon? Thank you very much. I'll say he has.' David chuckled. 'Not half.'

'What sort of things?' Eric asked it shyly—something about the holy ground of intimate pain inclining him to go on tiptoe in exploring it.

'Oh. . . .' Vagueness. David did not intend to be drawn. 'Maybe I'm saying more than I should. He's a private sort of chap. He's never talked to you about himself then?'

'No, not really. Before all this, I can't say we ever talked about, you know, personal things; and in the last few weeks he's been listening to me, I'm afraid. I've done all the talking. I must have been very selfish. He's looked after me splendidly.'

As he spoke the words, Eric realised that he was putting it all in the past tense. He was saying his thank yous for something which was over now. He was back on his feet. The worst was over.

Eric's pastor at Mount Grace noticed a returning of his old self, and so did his colleagues at school.

Eric began to resume the disciplines of Bible study and prayer again, and got to grips once more with the house-group study programme, which had wandered aimlessly through the first five chapters of First Corinthians over the preceding weeks. Other members of the group had taken over the preparation of the study material in the last few meetings, but Eric felt guilty that he had left the helm and let the ship drift for so long. They needed his leadership.

That Tuesday night he felt able to say to Simon, 'After tonight, don't feel you have to come to house group on my account. I shall be pleased, of course I will, if you feel you'd like to join us, but I can manage now.'

And for the first time for a long time, he sounded like himself as he led the opening prayer, and began the study: 'So, perhaps we can just run quickly through chapter six, which is about immoral living and food sacrificed to idols. I don't think there's anything to keep us talking especially, here.

'An interesting passage at the beginning which tells us not to take each other to court, to settle our differences among ourselves, which of course we should. Then this

long list of people who Paul says won't inherit the kingdom of God. Sounds a bit like a summarised reading of the
daily newspaper, doesn't it?'

He could feel his confidence returning as he spoke. It
wasn't the same as it had always been, of course it wasn't,
but he felt like a leader again. He was able to feel gratitude
instead of humiliation at the thought of their prayers.

'You'll notice that all the sins Paul mentions here are sins
that cause social breakdown, destroying trust, or destroying the family unit which is, of course, the God-ordained
basis of society. And indeed, research has borne this out, in
that every single civilisation has, in the early days of its
strength, revered and supported the concept of the family
unit. It is in each case a symptom or perhaps a cause of the
decline and fall of a civilisation when sexual immorality—
promiscuity, free love and all that—become normal. I have
to confess that I fear for our society today. I really do. Even
the church. In some parts of the church they're even considering allowing homosexuals into the ministry, and this
is a sign of our times. We should see things like AIDS as a
sign of God warning us, calling us back in his love before
it's too late.

'Sorry, Alice; were you wanting to ask a question?'

After this good beginning, a little twinge of dread made
itself felt in Eric's stomach at Alice Andrews' interruption.
Somewhere deep inside himself, Eric was afraid of Alice's
questions. She was a frank and intelligent person, and
Amy was the one who had usually dealt with some of
her more adventurous thoughts. But now there was no
Amy. Now Amy had taken her place in that shameful list
of people who shall not inherit the kingdom, cut off from
grace. Alice was speaking, and Eric was not listening. He
forced himself back to attention. He had to lead this thing
by himself now; he'd better be on the ball.

'. . . but what's wrong with being homosexual?'

Eric blinked at her. 'I'm dreadfully sorry, Alice. I missed the first part of your question.'

'I said, I can see how the other things in the list destroy trust and relationships between people, break down society, but what's wrong with being homosexual?'

Eric looked down at his Bible. His mind felt numb, dull. Those wretched pills.

'Well, it's just against the will of God,' he said. 'It's not normal. It breaks down the family unit. Homosexuals can't have children.'

'But you and Amy couldn't have children.'

The other people in the room shifted uncomfortably. Amy was still taboo for conversation. But Eric looked steadily at Alice.

'No,' he said, 'but we would have liked to have had children. And we didn't know we couldn't when we got married.'

'So what does that mean?' Alice persisted. 'Do you mean if you'd known you couldn't have children you wouldn't have married her? Anyway, perhaps some homosexuals would like to have children.'

An indefinable air of hostility was hardening towards Alice in the group. Questioning that included mention of Amy was definitely below the belt.

Jean Kirkwood raised her head from her scrutiny of the Bible, an unfamiliar light of battle in her mild brown eyes.

'What are you wanting us to believe, Alice?' she demanded. 'Of course homosexuality is wrong. It's right here in this list along with swindling and slandering. It's a sign of our moral decay in society that it's allowed by law now. It used to be the case that homosexuals went to prison, to punish them for doing indecent things and interfering with little children, and it's my belief they still should. In a God-fearing society, a sin should be the same thing as a crime.'

Eric opened his mouth to speak, but Alice got in before him.

'Oh, don't be so stupid!' she responded, hotly.

Jean's face went pink and she glared at Alice. Eric drew breath again, but Alice was still going.

'People still *do* go to prison for interfering with little children, and most of those are heterosexual. Homosexuals don't do indecent things, they just make love. That's no more indecent than me and Richard making love! Granted, some can be promiscuous, and I don't agree with that, but I don't agree with heterosexual promiscuity either. It's exactly the same.'

'Alice—' Eric felt he had to stop her before this erupted into a row.

'I think it's just old Paul and his sex hang-ups that got homosexuality into this list at all. You won't find anything about it in the Gospels. For all we know, Jesus might have been gay. Or married.'

'*Alice*!' She stopped abruptly, head held high and nostrils flared like a wild horse. Never mind the fabric of society. Alice was set fair to destroy the fabric of this house group if Eric didn't get it back on course. It just showed what could happen if people were left for any length of time without a firm pastoral lead.

'Of course Jesus wasn't gay,' he said calmly. 'And he wasn't married either.' He put up his hand to quell her impetuous interruption.

'You can't just dismiss the word of God as "old Paul and his sex hang-ups". Remember, the question you should be asking yourself is not, "Do I agree with this book?" but, "Does this book agree with me?"'

'Well in that case,' (Eric allowed her this final shot) 'women should be veiled from head to foot and we shouldn't eat prawns.'

Eric gazed at her wearily. Whatever was she on about? He couldn't get his brain round it somehow. He was still too slow. It had all taken too much out of him. He glanced across at Simon. It was a shame that he had been here to hear this wrangling. Whatever must he think? Amy would never have let it happen. Oh, why had she had to go?

'Can I say something?' Richard Andrews was altogether a more peaceful soul than his new wife. He blinked behind his thick glasses like a kindly and rather sleepy owl. Eric smiled at him encouragingly.

'Well, funnily enough, I've just been reading a book about this. In my book, it says that, um, homosexual acts in New and Old Testament times often took place in the context of promiscuous goings-on connected with pagan religions—um, orgies and prostitution and whatnot. It might be because of that that Paul was so down on it. The other thing, of course, is that the Jewish people were very concerned to protect their identity as the people of God, um, not allowing intermarriage you know; and to build up their race. Contraception was also a sin for them—um, "onanism", which is, er, spilling one's seed on the ground. Might it not be that the prohibition of homosexuality is of a similar *cultural* relevance—because, um, of course, as you so rightly point out, homosexuals aren't going to build up the race either? This may have reinforced the, er, sexual taboo surrounding it for the Jewish people, and caused it to seem particularly, um, abhorrent.'

'Well, I think that's just piffle.' James Stuart had been growing more and more restless in the corner, and could no longer control his impatience.

'I'm sorry, but I do. It seems to me that this is not an issue about homosexuality at all. It's about the Bible. Either you believe the Bible is the word of God, or you don't. If you do, then we understand each other. If you don't, then we simply have no dialogue. And if you believe in the Bible as the word of God, then it's quite simple: two and two simply make four. The Bible says that homosexuality is a sin, so it is a sin. You either believe it or you don't.'

Eric was about to grasp this lifeline with gratitude, when Richard Andrews began again.

'I take your point, er, James, but I'm not convinced it's quite so simple. Might it not be that the Bible, as it were, um, *contains* the word of God, but buried and intertwined with, er, cultural accretions, appropriate to its, um, contemporary pastoral setting?

'I myself see it rather like a jigsaw puzzle. Um, when you look at it whole, the face of God emerges, but the separated bits don't, um, well, they don't show you anything much.'

Janet Lewis, who had been sitting looking bemused until now, leaned forward to speak.

'Of course we can't have homosexual ministers,' she said. 'Not practising homosexuals. Apart from anything else, they can't get married, can they? So even if it was all right to be homosexual, it wouldn't be all right, would it, because they wouldn't be married?'

'Oh, I don't believe it!' Alice muttered, rudely, but Janet was not put off.

'I've been a widow for seventeen years now, and sometimes I would have liked to go to bed with someone—yes I would.' She was blushing, and talking rather fast, but she was brave enough to continue. 'But I haven't done, because that's forbidden fruit for me. And if I'm not allowed to taste forbidden fruit, why should homosexuals be?'

Most members of the group nodded thoughtfully. Simon still had his head down looking into his Bible. Alice was shaking her head impatiently.

'But Janet, before you were widowed you were married for twenty years. That's twenty years you didn't have to be celibate in. And you might get married again. But you're saying that all homosexuals have to be celibate for ever, which is not the same at all.'

Janet looked at her. 'If a practising homosexual came to

be the minister of Mount Grace,' she said, 'I would leave. I would have to. I believe in upholding scriptural principle, I'm afraid, Alice. I don't mind discussing points of view, but when it comes down to the way I live my life, I live by the Bible.'

'Um, yes.' Richard was back into the fray. 'But all of us read the Bible, um, *interpretatively*. For example, you at this moment are, um, choosing to ignore my interpretation in favour of your own. In the same way, it is quite possible for, um, a practising homosexual to live his or her life by the Bible, um, according to his or her own interpretation.'

'No.' Jean Kirkwood was shaking her head. 'No. I'm sorry, Richard, but you're wrong. Besides, if you let one homosexual in, he might seduce the young people into his way of thinking. How could you let a homosexual work with the Youth Fellowship? You never know what might happen!'

'Can we move on now?' Eric had had enough of this. 'I think we've probably discussed this in enough depth. We must bear in mind that our studies are on the theme of Christian Character, and although it may be quite interesting to touch on the subject of homosexuality, it's a bit of a deviation really, because I don't think it has much to do with the character of a Christian—'

'Not even a Christian homosexual?' butted in Alice. Eric frowned in irritation, and continued, '—so if there's anything else in that list anyone wants to discuss, we could have a look at that, and then move on.'

'Yes, there is.' Alice again. Eric looked at her in disbelief. For a moment, he almost hated her.

'There is. After "thieves" in this list of sinners comes "usurers". The Bible says that usury, lending money at exorbitant interest, is a sin. Well, surely our whole society is built on usury. Surely any of us who have investments, or money in the bank are involved in usury. Like the world debt: countries where people are starving and paying us more in interest repayments than we send them in aid. Any of us who have   savings, or maybe even if we have a mortgage or use a bank at all, are implicated in that. It seems a bit hypocritical to say homosexuals can't be ministers on the basis of what it says here, and then let people involved in usury, which is in the same list, into the pulpit.'

'Thank you, Alice,' said Eric heavily, 'for your considerable contribution to our discussion. And now perhaps we can move on?'

By the end of the evening, Eric felt utterly drained. He put the kettle on for a fresh cup of coffee as Simon stood washing up at the sink.

The two men sat down together at the kitchen table with their mugs of coffee.

'This kitchen's been the scene of some rare old struggles these last few weeks,' said Eric.

Simon nodded. 'Yes,' he said. Eric glanced at him. He seemed very quiet—well, he was always quiet, but a bit withdrawn. Eric sighed. Probably he didn't think much of all that carry-on in the house-group meeting.

'Look, I'm sorry about this evening,' Eric said, hesitantly.

Simon looked across at him, didn't speak for a moment. Then, 'Why?' he asked, cautiously.

'Well, you know. These things are better understood by the pastoral team really. People like Alice Andrews can be an absolute menace. I sometimes think she just lives to make trouble.'

Simon looked down into his coffee, swilled it round his cup thoughtfully. 'I thought what she said was quite helpful,' he said. His voice was very quiet.

Eric felt the same constricting anxiety he used to feel when Amy was upset. He had never understood properly when Amy was upset; never said the right things, always put his foot in it. He had an awful feeling the same thing was going to happen now. There was something bothering Simon, and it made Eric feel helpless, clumsy. He thought perhaps if he continued the conversation, it would draw Simon out, give a lead somewhere.

'Oh, well, yes, she certainly keeps us all thinking!' he said. 'But of course, we have to remember that it's not what we think, it's what the Bible says that counts. Bit of an unsavoury topic really, wasn't it? Still, we have to be realistic, face up to the real world, don't we? After all, there are plenty of them out there, needing God's people to show them the way out of their sin.'

Simon put his cup down. 'Plenty of who?' he asked.

'Sinners—prostitutes, drug addicts, homosexuals. Cut off from the grace of God.'

Simon drew up one knee to his chest, and sat awkwardly huddled in the chair, hugging himself protectively. His face was twisted into a curious little smile, and he gazed past Eric, thinking, weighing his reply. Once he drew breath to speak, and Eric waited for the words, but they did not come. Eric couldn't think what on earth was the matter with him.

Then, with impatient resolution, Simon abandoned his defensive shrinking, and sat up straight in the chair. Level and direct, very bright, his eyes met Eric's.

'The thing is,' he said, 'when you say all those things, you're talking about me. I'm gay. You're talking about me.'

It is not often that a man's jaw literally drops— it is usually a figure of speech. But Eric's jaw dropped then. For a moment he gazed speechlessly at Simon, his eyes boggling in blank amazement. Simon looked back at him, resigned, amused, defensive, all at the same time.

'Do you mean . . .?' Eric fought his way back to a form of speech at last. Simon raised his eyebrows enquiringly. Then a new horror crystallised in Eric's eyes as he stared at the different form of life Simon had just become.

'David—he. . . . Are you and he—? He's not—? Is David your *lover*?'

If Eric had been a man who listened to such things, he

would have heard the curious hush in Simon's voice as he replied. If he had been looking for it, and interested, he would have looked into Simon's eyes, and realised that in that moment he was privileged to meet honesty and courage in naked form.

'Yes,' Simon replied.

But that was not what Eric was looking for. He had his mind on other things.

'Do you mean that when he—ugh!—that when he comes here you—? Here? In my house? Without my consent?'

Simon received his outraged glare quietly.

'I'm sorry,' he said. 'I thought that when it said consenting adults, it was David's consent I had to have, not yours.'

'But this is *my house*!'

'Well, we didn't do anything to the house. I mean we didn't swing from the light fittings or stain the sheets or anything.'

Eric's eyes bulged. 'Is that it? Is that all you can say?'

'I'm sorry. You. . . . Look, David and I, we love each other, that's all. We make love. He's my partner. We love each other. I didn't tell you because—well because I knew I'd have to go through all this, and because I thought you might throw me out if you knew. And because,' he added softly, 'it's really none of your business.'

He would have left it there. He was mindful of the fact that Eric was still in a vulnerable state; had scarcely got back his equilibrium to face the problems he already had.

'It's late, Eric,' he said. 'Let's talk it over some other time. Maybe I shouldn't have said anything.'

Eric, however, was having none of this. 'Now just hang on,' he replied. 'I don't think we can just leave it there. You can't drop a bombshell like that, and just expect to walk away from the consequences.'

'I'm not walking away. I—'

'I was wondering why you were so jolly quiet. Don't you think you should have mentioned this before?'

'Oh, God, you remind me of my father. I liked you better before you got back into your stride as an elder of the church. There's a nice man underneath that Pharisee.'

Eric glared at him indignantly. Simon shrugged his shoulders and looked away.

'Oh, all right then,' Simon said into the bristling silence between them. 'Don't let's fight. You're my friend. Maybe I shouldn't have kept so quiet. Maybe I should have spoken up in the house group. I thought you had enough to cope with as it was.

'The way I look at it is that anyone can have an opinion. If you think AIDS is the wrath of God and buggery is sin too heinous to mention, well, fine. That's your opinion. I can take that. But what I can't take is that, so far as I can see, in your church opinions aren't allowed. Or at least, only your opinions, not mine. That's a kind of spiritual Nazism, isn't it? Annihilate a person's gay identity by counselling and brainwashing it out of existence. Use all the influence and political leverage at your command to exclude from power in the church all those with a different sexuality, a different theology, a different gender from your own.

'That's what Hitler wanted: to create a world in which there was nothing left to even *remind* him of a different point of view. And if that's what your God wants, good luck to him, but I don't worship that kind of God. In my world, the people are all different, and my God can live with that. My Jesus is the Jesus who says to Martha, "Clear off! Leave Mary alone! If she wants to get stuck into theology, well I like that. She'll be better in the pulpit than she is in the kitchen."

'My Jesus is the Jesus who tells the story of the Good Samaritan, and then asks the racist Pharisee, "And which of these was the man's neighbour?" And the Pharisee can't get round it. He has to say, "It was the one who showed him kindness. It was the heretic whom I spit on the street at the sight of. It was the one there is no room for in my world."

'And Jesus says, "That's right. Well you go and be like that heretic, because he was the one who had it right." Apoplectic, that Pharisee must have been.

'I'll tell you something, Eric. I love Jesus. Right from the middle of me, I love Jesus. I love him because he loves me the way I am. I love him because he searches me and knows me. He looks right into me and *he loves me*. He's no damned Nazi God who looks at me and says there isn't room for people like me in the world. He loves me. OK?'

Eric cleared his throat, cautiously feeling his way into a reply.

'Of course God loves you, Simon. Of course he loves you as you are. But maybe he doesn't want you to *stay* as you are? Perhaps he wants to heal you of your homosexuality. Perhaps he wants to love your potential into being. Just *because* he loves you he isn't satisfied with anything less than the best for you.'

Simon took a deep breath. 'Look,' he said, struggling to maintain a rational restraint, 'I don't believe my homosexuality is a sin, or an illness. But let's suppose just for a minute it is. Are there not ministers in the church who have illnesses? Diabetes, say. Are there not ministers who sin—deceitful ministers, ministers who cruelly neglect their children, ministers who treat their wives as unpaid drudges, ministers who use their vocation as a focus of proud ambition, climbing the career structures of the church? Aren't there lazy ministers, greedy ministers? And you can live with them, can't you? But a woman or a homosexual in the pulpit—you can't live with that!'

Eric sighed. 'The issue of women's ordination is another story altogether. Let's leave that for tonight—it's getting late. Simon, I believe in the Bible teaching. The Bible teaches that homosexuality is wrong.'

'Does it? Perhaps you were thinking of the lascivious

young men of Sodom who gathered round Lot's house
and tried to force him to throw out his male guests for
them to rape? Well, you may be encouraged to know that I
don't approve of rape either. In fact I'm not very impressed
by the reaction of Lot, the righteous man, who offered to
throw his virgin daughters to the rapists so as to let his
guests off the hook.

'Or maybe you were thinking of the teaching of St Paul,
who taught that homosexuals couldn't enter the kingdom
of heaven, and that women should be silent in church and
wear veils, and that it was OK to keep a slave?

'Eric, last week David told me you'd said to him that
I'd been like Jesus to you. I was very touched. Thank you.
Perhaps you could just be content to meet Jesus where
you didn't expect to find him, and to love him in his
unexpected disguise.'

Eric said nothing. It was late. He felt tired and muddled.

'It's wrong,' he said, doggedly, at last. 'The Bible says it's
wrong. But you were—you *were* like Jesus to me.'

Simon nodded. 'What I want,' he said, 'is for you to
allow me the dignity of my own point of view. I don't
agree with you, but I accept your morality. I don't want
to drum you out of the church, or silence you, or have you
counselled until you see things like me. I don't want to
change your sexuality to make it like mine. There's room in
God's church for both of us. What I want is that you should
extend the same degree of acceptance to me.'

'But Simon, the Bible is the word of God,' said Eric. 'You
can't pick and choose with it, and you can't ignore it. The
book of Deuteronomy condemns homosexuality as the
same kind of thing as prostitution, and—'

'I know. And the letter to the Romans says those who
practise such things deserve to die; and the letter to the
Corinthians says people like me will never enter the kingdom of heaven. I know, Eric; I've read it. Read it and reread
it and laid awake at night thinking about it, and cried

myself to sleep over it. And what am I to do? It's what I *am*. It's not just something I do, like a hobby. It's what I am.'

'Perhaps . . . maybe God wants to change you?'

'Change me? Eric, we're not talking about a little foible here, a personality quirk, a penchant for the boys. My *whole being*—God wants to change my whole being?'

'Yes. Yes. If you believe the Bible. Yes.'

After a little silence, Simon asked him, softly, 'So then . . . who will I be?'

'Well, I don't know . . .' Eric felt uncomfortable; Simon's eyes were fixed on him, and there was a deep unhappiness looking out of them that he felt somehow responsible for. His efforts so far didn't seem to resemble a healing miracle very much.

'Maybe,' Eric ventured, 'you should just trust God to change you.'

'Into what?' Simon asked again. 'Somebody like you? Please don't think too badly of me if I decline the offer. I'm not setting myself up as a saint, Eric, but no thanks. I don't want to be like you. And I think I'd like to stop this conversation now.'

The whole thing was more than Eric could take. He went to bed uneasy, and the next Monday, having talked things over on Sunday night with his pastor, he reluctantly asked Simon to find another place to stay.

He read again the passage from 1 Corinthians urging Christians not to associate with sexually immoral people— not even to eat with them; to drive the wicked one out of the community. He felt like a traitor doing it, but he reminded himself that as an elder and house-group leader, it was his responsibility to stand by Christian principles. He knew he couldn't look Simon in the eye and say it, though. He had to leave him a note on the kitchen table, explaining and asking him to go.

He was relieved that Simon didn't make a fuss; there

were no recriminations. All he said was, 'Will you give me till next week to find somewhere?'

With the effusiveness of relief, Eric had assured him that that would be all right. That week, Simon was out every evening. Eric had to do the grocery shopping by himself.

The following Wednesday, David came to help Simon move his belongings. Anxious, apologetic, Eric buttonholed him in the kitchen.

'He'll be all right? He'll be able to stay with you for a while?'

'Oh yes,' said David, 'though I would hardly have thought you'd see that as a moral improvement! He'll be all right. He's used to people like you.' He hesitated, then said, 'There's something I'd like to say to you, though.'

Without waiting for a reply, he continued, 'One day, make no mistake, Jesus will say to you: "I was in need of your friendship, but you would only offer me your cold morality. I put myself in your hands, and you threw me away. I was gay, so you showed me the street." And then I guess he'll say to you, "Grow up, Eric. That's not the gospel."'

THREE SHORT PIECES

These pieces can be used in a different way from the other, longer, stories. They arrest the attention, make people stop, think, look again; a challenge to see beyond surfaces and think beyond assumptions.

The Dolly is a two-minute piece—the right length for a 'Thought for the Day'. It can be used as a children's address, or in a situation where you are given a tiny 'God-slot', just a couple of minutes to communicate the gospel in a nutshell. Because it is written for that sort of wide, anonymous audience, it has been carefully worded to avoid religious sensitivities, and is suitable for an audience of non-Christians, to give a flavour of the kind of God we believe in, and an accessible introduction to some theological concepts of sin (having fallen, being lost).

Tulip and the Boating Party was written as an opening piece to begin a period of intercessions, and it can be used as a meditation in a short opening devotion to begin a meeting or discussion group. The intercessions that went with *Tulip and the Boating Party* are given at the end of the story.

Chance Meeting would be used in a similar way to

Tulip, and I have used it on a broadsheet which included quotations from the Bible (eg, Isaiah 58:1–12; Luke 6:20–26) and from various writers (Jean Vanier, Helder Camara, Mother Teresa, etc) to stimulate thought and discussion of Christian response to homelessness.

The Dolly

'Do you see this woman?' (Luke 7:44, NIV)

The Dolly

As a child, accompanying my mother on shopping expeditions around department stores in London's West End, I entertained myself by keeping a sharp eye out for buttons or coins or other interesting dropped things. The habit has stuck, and to this day I tend to walk down the road with one eye to the pavement and what it may have to offer.

The town where I live, like others, has its fair share of litter blowing about its streets, and one day I almost walked past what I took to be a twisted, discarded, coloured sweet paper, like those shiny foil and cellophane toffee wrappers. But something about it arrested my attention, made my footsteps pause. I was seized with the irresistible impression that this little scrap of rubbish on the street was a person. Somehow, in its form, was that which I recognised. I bent down and picked it up. Sure enough, to my fascination and delight, it *was* a person: a tiny dolly, no bigger than a sweet wrapper, accidentally fallen and lost; a little image of humanity which had called out to me and stopped me as I walked by. I put her carefully in my purse and took her home. I keep her still.

I like to think that however small and insignificant I may be; however low I may have fallen, even to the gutter;

however lost I may be, degraded to rubbish, abandoned, voiceless, helpless; the great God of heaven passing by will pause, and stooping down will pick me up and carry me home, keep me always, recognising in my lostness the unerasable image of God's own self.

Tulip and the Boating Party

Speak, yourself, on behalf of the dumb,
  on behalf of all the unwanted;
speak, yourself, pronounce a just verdict,
  uphold the rights of the poor, of the needy (Prov 31:8–9).

Tulip and the Boating Party

A party of six friends had hired a rowing-boat and set out together down-river. They were all married couples from the same town. Some were old school-friends, some were members of the Rotary Club and the Amateur Dramatic Society. They liked each others' company, and spent a lot of time together, often planning outings like this.

It was early in the day, and though it felt pleasantly warm out, patches of mist still clung about the bushes and weeping willows and reeds that overhung the river banks, shrouding the dark, tugging water with mystery.

A strong current helped the boat's progress along the river. Getting back would be the real muscle-builder.

Suddenly, Tulip, one of the party, startled everybody by jumping to her feet. The boat tipped perilously. Tulip's husband nearly dropped the sculls, and he cried out crossly: 'Sit down, Tulip! You're rocking the boat!'

But Tulip did not sit down.

'Look!' she exclaimed, pointing: 'There's someone in trouble! Look! Can't you hear him calling? Look! Can't you see him?'

From where she stood balancing precariously in the swaying boat, Tulip could see a lonely figure in the mist near the willow trees, waving frantically, calling, 'Help! Please help me! I can't swim!'

He was not so far away. She could see the fear and the plea in his eyes.

'Oh God, help me! Please help me! I can't swim!'

'Turn back!' Tulip cried out urgently. 'Quick! There's someone in trouble!'

But to her consternation, her friends in the boat replied, 'Oh, come off it, Tulip; there's nobody there. Sit down! You'll have *us* in the water if you're not careful, and none of us can swim.'

'But . . . there's someone in distress . . .' Tulip faltered a little, puzzled. Had she imagined it, that they seemed so unconcerned?

'Yes, there *is*,' she insisted, as she listened again. He had gone under for a moment, but she could see him again now.

'*We* can't hear anybody,' her friends replied, getting a bit irritable with her now.

'There's nobody there.

And if there is, he's not one of us.

And if he is, the boat's full anyway.

And if it wasn't, it would be too difficult to turn back now.

Sit down, Tulip. You're rocking the boat.'

Then Tulip was torn two ways. She was sure she had not imagined that desperate, struggling figure in the water, and the fear in his eyes and his voice. But as she peered back into the mist, nothing disturbed the water there but wide ripples from the wake of their boat. There was nothing to hear but the rattle and splash of the sculls, and the quacking of a duck in the reeds.

And as she slowly sat down again, the icy possibility settled in her heart that he had drowned, because like them

he couldn't swim. They had left him to die and he had
died.

Or was it Tulip who died, and only the stranger who
lived on in the vault of her heart, crying out: 'Help me! Oh
God, help me! I can't swim!'?

Prayers of intercession

We remember before you, God, the ones we betrayed and
    left behind,
the ones we left struggling,
the ones whose voices cry out of the past, haunting us still.

We remember before you, God, the ones whose need calls
    out in our lives now,
the hands which reach out to us,
the eyes that look to us for help.

We remember with dearest thanks the ones who have come
    to our side in our own times of trouble,
the people who have been for us Emmanuel,
whose presence has healed us and been salvation to us.

We pray knowing that some of us here will be the
    struggling ones today,
the sinking ones crying out to God and to the community.
May we incarnate for each other the God who remembers
    us,
who does not turn away.

And we beg you, Living God, do not abandon us.
Do not take your Holy Spirit from us.

Chance Meeting

Is it nothing to you, all you who pass by? (Lamentations 1:12, NIV)

Chance Meeting

I hadn't expected—I mean, somehow, I never thought I'd find you here, like this. I knew that one day—well, that is to say, it seemed likely—no: more than that; I knew. I knew. I knew that one day I'd meet you face to face. But I thought there would be, well, you know, a long approach. I thought you'd call me, and my heart would thrill, and you would invite me, and maybe there would be a long, long strip of carpet (good quality, 100% wool, no dog hairs, no crumbs) and marble steps and a throne. And I thought—I thought you'd be . . . well . . . clean at the very least.

Oh, I suppose I should have known; you've been surprising me long enough.

I was coming round the corner to the station, out of breath, worried about missing the train. Just come out of one meeting, on my way to another. A long afternoon on social justice, housing, welfare benefits; then a train journey, then Worship Committee. I nearly got killed on the road, skipping out of the path of a car, horn blaring—aggressive man! I was tired and hungry, out of sorts.

Just time to grab a sandwich and a drink, phone home to let them know which train . . . Then I came past the flower stall and level with the café doorway, and there you were.

Sitting on a stuffed rucksack, dirty—I mean really grimy, all your clothes and your hair and everything. Two, three days maybe, since you had a shave. Your shoulders were hunched against the cold and damp. Tired, I would say, but (surprisingly) not defeated. You were looking up to talk to a nicely dressed elderly lady. She looked concerned, bending over you. She must have seen the grubby scrap of cardboard at your feet, saying: 'Homeless and hungry.'

When I saw you . . . I don't know, I . . . it was as though the whole world stopped. Just your face, unshaven, weary, the lady bending over you, the torn-off bit of cardboard 'Homeless and hungry' . . . homeless . . . hungry . . . still? *Still?* Hunched against the cold in a café doorway.

I had to get that train. Well, it was Worship Committee. I wanted . . . I thought I should . . . anyway, you were already talking to someone. She looked kind. I thought maybe she'd buy you something to eat. Something, I don't know.

Anyway, it was not what I was expecting. I've waited and watched long enough: hoping, wondering; but I thought. . . . Oh, the long and the short of it is, it wasn't till I was on the train, and I'd eaten my sandwich, and I was sitting looking at the commuters, so grey and drained at the end of the day, slumped in their seats, ties pulled loose to ease constricting collars, and I couldn't get you out of my mind . . . but I didn't . . . we were pulling in to East Croydon, and I suddenly realised . . . that memory of your face, tired, looking up to talk to a woman . . . woman at the well . . . woman bleeding . . . woman with a demented child . . . your face, intent, unshaven . . . so grimy . . . not until we were pulling in to East Croydon that I realised . . . your face—oh, God! It was *Jesus!* And by then it was too late.

STUDY NOTES

Study Notes

Every small group that meets together is different, and the Notes that follow are only meant to be guidelines. I hope that you will adapt them to suit the people in your group.

I always assume that the group will start with a cup of coffee and a chat. In a fellowship group, people want not only to study and learn and think, they also want to meet each other, to affirm each other's humanity by being comfortable and sociable together. This coffee time is of great value, enabling friendships to be developed, new people to be welcomed and lonely people to be loved.

Having said that, all good things must come to an end, and people like something to get their teeth into besides biscuits, so keep the coffee time fairly strictly to about twenty minutes—fifteen if there is a lot to get through. This is long enough for greeting and gossip, and anyone who wants to take two hours telling you all their troubles can burn the midnight oil with you when the group has gone home, or else make another date.

Some of the suggestions that follow are for the whole group, and some recommend splitting into small groups. If your group is six people or less, only split them if they are comfortable with each other. A small group is six or less, a large group (referred to as 'the whole group') is six or more.

It is important that the leader should set an example in listening properly to each person, helping them to feel that what they have to say is interesting, but at the same time trying not to allow people who find it easy to put things into words to monopolise the air space.

I have suggested a short devotion to finish each study. If you feel this is not appropriate for your group, then perhaps you could just use the suggested prayers, but do try to finish your time together with an opportunity for quiet and reflection.

Study Notes for In Grosvenor Street

This is a very simple story, which makes one basic point: that Jesus was a real human being like you and me. It is also quite a short story, taking only about twenty minutes to read aloud. These things make it suitable for use in place of a sermon, especially on a winter evening when the lamps are lit and people are in story mood. It can also be used as a Holy Week address, in one of the special services, as a change from sermons. It enables people to relate to the cross and Passion of Jesus in a direct, uncomplicated way, and to celebrate his utter humanity, which is crucial to the goodness of the good news.

In Grosvenor Street can also be used as a house-group study text, and various things can be drawn out of it for that. Because it is a simple, short, very non-threatening story, it is a gentle beginning for using fiction with a house group.

It could be used as a starter for a discussion about suffering. In the story, Dai Richards thinks about Jesus as a young man like his own son Ceri. Dai's relationship with his son is both painful and loving. How can the suffering of Jesus give us strength and inspiration in our own troubles?

The story is woven around the theme of parenthood,

which nobody finds easy. Here is an opportunity for us to look at our own family experiences, to share memories and uncertainties, and learn a bit about one another's backgrounds and lives.

There are lots of possibilities, but here is the outline of a study you might like to follow.

If appropriate, ask the people in your group the week before the study session to try to find a picture of Jesus and also a way in which the Bible describes Jesus (eg, Shepherd, the Way, the Door, Messiah, etc).

Look up some of the words/titles/images the group has found in the New Testament to describe Jesus. When you have looked up as many as you want to, ask which ones people find it easy to relate to, and which ones seem baffling or unattractive.

(15–20 mins)

Now break into small groups of up to six people. In each group either invite everyone to show the pictures they have brought, encouraging each person to talk a little bit about the picture, or invite them to describe and speak about a picture of Jesus they can remember, or how they themselves picture Jesus.

(20–30 mins)

If your group was big enough to split up into small groups, come back together now. Ask each group for anything that came out of their small group time that they specially want to share with the whole group.

(5–10 mins)

Introduce the story now, by explaining that this story shows how one man came to understand something more about Jesus by relating the Jesus pictured in the

New Testament, and the Jesus he had seen (in his case, a statue), to his own life.

(3 mins)

Read the story *In Grosvenor Street*.

(20 mins)

Invite the group to share their responses to the story, with questions such as:

- Did it offer you any new understanding about Jesus?
- Did the story spark off any particular memory or train of thought for you?
- Was the picture of Jesus the story offered you similar to or very different from the pictures described by the group?

Again, remember to give people time to speak and share, and proper attention so they feel listened to and are not interrupted.

(17 mins)

Closing devotions

Songs

When I survey the wondrous cross
Amazing grace
I cannot tell why He, whom angels worship
Hallelujah, my Father
You laid aside Your majesty

Readings

'God loved the world so much that he gave his only Son, so that everyone who believes in him may not be lost but may have eternal life. For God sent his Son into the world not to condemn the world, but so that through him the world might be saved' (Jn 3:16–17).

'God wanted all perfection to be found in him and all things to be reconciled through him and for him, everything in heaven and everything on earth, when he made peace by his death on the cross' (Col 1: 19–20).

Prayer

For Jesus, our Friend and our Brother,
we thank you, loving God.
For the way he loved us without counting the cost
we thank you, loving God.
The grace you have given us
freely, generously,
in the life of Jesus,
is our salvation, our healing, our hope.
Take our lives and shape them in his image
so that we too may truly be
the citizens of your kingdom,
the children of your family,
the heirs of your grace.   Amen.

(10 mins)

Summary

Coffee	15–20 mins
Whole group	15–20 mins
Small groups	20–30 mins
Feedback	5–10 mins
Introduction to story	3 mins
Story	20 mins (approx)

Responses to story	17 mins
Devotions	10 mins
Total time	105–130 mins

Suitable for a 7.30–9.30pm house-group meeting or any other two-hour meeting.

Study Notes for Time to Put Things Right

This story takes about twenty minutes, or a little more, to read, which makes it suitable to use in place of a sermon, or to read to your house group during a meeting. If your study group meets on a Sunday evening, one possibility is to use this story in place of the sermon in your evening church service, and then the study could follow on afterwards.

It is a simple story, exploring themes of forgiveness, acceptance, honesty and facing up to our difficulties. How demanding it is of the group will depend mainly on how much the leader encourages them towards considering their own struggles rather than those of other people.

Two approaches using this story as a basis for study are:

1. *Home and family.* The questions here are:

Family life can be a safe and loving environment, or it can be hell on earth. What has the church to say to those homeless people who have left their homes because they found life there intolerable?

Do we do right in placing so much emphasis on 'the family' at church (family values, family services, etc)? How might single people and those whose family life is a nightmare feel about this?

What experiences of home and family are there within the study group? Is there a willingness to share problems encountered, experiences of facing up to broken relationships, financial troubles, fear of responsibility, etc?

2. *Sacramental relationships.* A sacrament is defined as 'an outward and visible sign of an inward and invisible truth'. In other words, it is when something you can touch, taste and see leads you to God who is truth but whom you can't touch, taste or see.

We call the Lord's Supper a sacrament, but in some ways much of life is sacramental if we let it be.

In this story you may notice that in the passages describing the two men spending time together, reference is made to the breaking of bread and the giving of a cup, which is done to evoke resonances of a sacramental meal, guiding the reader's imagination towards the understanding that in this relationship, this 'communion', the presence of God will be found.

In the study outline that follows, the second option, 'sacramental relationships', is the one I am choosing to explore.

In the whole group listen to the story *Time to Put Things Right.*

(25 mins)

Take a few minutes to sit quietly and let the story sink in. Invite the group to share any particular impressions or thoughts the story may have sparked off.

(10 mins)

In small groups (if appropriate), think about one or more of the following questions, and share your thoughts together.

• Can you remember a time in your life when something happened, or someone said or did something, and it seemed almost as if they were an angel—one of those people of whom we say 'he or she was Jesus to me'?

- Often when we have problems in our lives, things become more and more of a tangle, and we need to be able to talk them through with someone. It is very difficult to admit honestly what we are like on the inside. It can make us feel very afraid that the person will despise us, and we can be afraid of crying, or just very ashamed. What sort of person would someone need to be for you to trust them with the truth about yourself? Or maybe you can't imagine trusting anyone that much?

- When someone has come to you and told you his or her troubles in this way, maybe admitted something he or she had done wrong, told you what a mess everything was, how did you feel about that person?

(20 mins)

In the whole group look up James 5:16: '. . . confess your sins to one another, and pray for one another, and this will cure you.'

And John 8:11: '"Neither do I condemn you," said Jesus. "Go away, and don't sin any more."'

And Mark 2:1–12, the story of the paralysed man, looking especially at these words in verses 9–11:

> 'Which of these is easier: to say to the paralytic, "Your sins are forgiven", or to say, "Get up, pick up your stretcher and walk"? But to prove to you that the Son of Man has authority on earth to forgive sins,'—he said to the paralytic—'I order you: get up, pick up your stretcher, and go off home.'

There are many connections made in the gospels between healing and forgiveness and salvation.

Sin, sadness, hurting and illness all interfere with a person's wellbeing, and the good news of Jesus is the arrival of God's *shalom*—wholeness and peace.

Often people with illnesses came to Jesus asking, 'Can you cure me?' When he did, he would use the term 'made whole' rather than 'cured'. Translators have had trouble knowing how to render that word in English, because it means both 'saved' and 'healed'.

The 'salve' we put on a graze or wound is not unconnected with the 'salvation' that Jesus offers us. There is also a word St Luke uses to describe people who have 'gone astray'. It is 'lost' (the prodigal son, the lost sheep, Zaccheus).

The story *Time to Put Things Right* tries to weave together the concepts of sin, lostness and hurting/dis-ease, to show how the loving acceptance of Jesus brings a healing which answers the need of a person in all its complexity.

Spend some time looking at the Bible passages and discussing these ideas in your group. Something of the thoughts people shared in the small groups will be relevant to bring into this discussion.

(40 mins)

Closing devotions

For this, each person will need a pencil and a small piece of paper. You will also need either a fireplace (preferably with a fire in it) or a large dish in which the scraps of paper can be burned.

To 'confess' means to acknowledge or declare something—like when we go through Customs: 'Have you anything to declare?'

In our prayers of confession, we acknowledge or declare to the God who loves us and whom we can trust to go on loving us, what we really are.

Tonight, let's ask ourselves, in the privacy of our own hearts: 'Have I anything to declare to God?'

Maybe, as we look inside, we will find a memory of something we did wrong, and are ashamed of, and want forgiveness for. Maybe we will find a secret sore place, something someone said or did that bruised us, and the memory sticks. Maybe we will find a new sense of trust in God or in each other—a feeling of wellbeing, of feeling loved.

So let us silently ask the question: 'Have I anything to declare to God?' and write down what we find in our hearts on our pieces of paper.

Because we can't touch or see God, we will do what children do with letters to Father Christmas, putting their letters in the fire, to be magically carried to him. And this is a sacramental thing to do. It is an outward and visible sign of the inward and invisible truth that God hears and sees and knows who we are, how we are, and what we want to declare to the God who loves us.

(The group then takes a little time to write on the pieces of paper, which are then collected and burned.)

Reading

'It is by grace that you have been saved, through faith; not by anything of your own, but by a gift from God; not by anything that you have done, so that nobody can claim the credit. We are God's work of art, created in Christ Jesus to live the good life as from the beginning he had meant us to live it' (Eph 2:8–10).

Prayer

God of gentleness and mercy
In you is our healing, our hope and our strength.
Help us to be honest with you and with one another.
In our lives together,
may we reflect the patience and the kindness of Jesus,
in listening,
in understanding,
in refusing to condemn.

May the mercy and forgiveness you have shown to us
shine from our lives as a witness
of the presence
of your Holy Spirit in our hearts,
the starting point of our relationships with each other.
Amen.

Songs

O, let the Son of God enfold you
Here, O my Lord, I see Thee face to face
Be still and know that I am God—the version with three
    verses as given in *Songs of Fellowship* (Kingsway).

(15 mins)

Summary

Coffee	20 mins
Story	25 mins
Response	10 mins
Discussion in small groups	20 mins
Bible study and discussion	40 mins
Closing devotions	15 mins
Total time	130 mins

Suitable for a 7.30–9.30pm meeting.

Study Notes for Release

This story takes about twenty minutes to read, which means it can comfortably be read as part of a house-group meeting. The content of the story, however, makes it unsuitable to be used instead of a sermon in a formal worship setting in all but the most unusual churches.

Release explores themes of freedom and imprisonment, and also considers the culture clash between the world Jesus died for and the church that bears his name.

This story will require of your house group a sense of humour and a willingness to see themselves as others see them. If your group is a bit strait-laced, this is not the story for them.

In the whole group read the story.

(25 mins)

Sit quietly for a few minutes to consider the story you have just heard. As you are thinking, ask yourself the questions:

- Who was in prison in the story?

- What were the prisons?

(5 mins)

The whole group shares immediate thoughts and responses.

(15 mins)

Divide into small groups (if appropriate) to consider some of the following questions.

- How did you respond to the characters in the story? Who did you warm to and who didn't you like? Can you say why? Did the characters in the story remind you of anyone you know?

- What kind of God was Helen's God . . . Mike's God . . . Sue's God . . . Jim's God?

- Does it upset you when people swear? Why?

- How would you feel if Jim turned up at your house group? Or if everybody at your house group is like Jim, how would you feel if Helen turned up?

- Why do you think Sue was so relieved she didn't have to look after Helen's children?

- Do you find it threatening or frightening to be with people who are drunk? What are your views about drinking alcohol?

- Attitudes, prejudices and fear can keep people as much in prison as locked doors and razor-wire fences. Are there any such imprisoning attitudes that your own church or group needs to face?

(20 mins)

Come back together in the whole group, and feed back some of the thoughts that have been aired in the small groups. Allow a further period of time for discussion.

(30 mins)

Closing devotions

Songs

Set my spirit free, that I might worship Thee
There's a wideness in God's mercy

Readings

'All that the Father gives me will come to me, and whoever comes to me I shall not turn him away' (Jn 6:37).

Read the parable of the Pharisee and the publican (Lk 18:9–14).

Prayer

Holy Spirit of truth,
sent by Jesus to set us free,
please come down upon us in your gentle power.
Breathe into our hearts the love which casts out fear;
liberate us from stuffiness and prejudice.
Give us the grace to show others how to live
by the example of our lives.
May our faith be honest and real,
a human thing of kindness and laughter.
Remind us that we follow the one who came
not to condemn the world,
but that through him the world might be saved.
We offer you all our pious Pharisaism.
Please will you swap it for your abundant life,
for the sake of Jesus,
whose ambassadors we are supposed to be.   Amen.

Songs

I will rejoice in You and be glad
Give me oil in my lamp
Oh happy day

(10 mins)

Summary

Coffee	15 mins
Story	25 mins
Thinking time	5 mins
Responses	15 mins
Small groups	20 mins
Whole group discussion	30 mins
Devotions	10 mins
Total time	120 mins

Suitable for a 7.30–9.30pm meeting.

Study Notes for The Perfect Host

The Perfect Host is an exploration of sacramental theology and the Eucharist. Religion is often applied externally to our lives, as an antibiotic is to an infection, to do good to our fallen nature, to redeem us from the distasteful reality of our present state of being. That is why most religious people still feel guilty most of the time. In the Catholic world, the prime medicine is Holy Communion—the receiving of the sanctifying bread (the host) and wine. In the Protestant tradition, there are other medicines— ritualistic prayers of repentance following altar calls, for example.

This story looks at that sacramental cleansing from a different point of view. It takes the word 'host', and uses it to present another way of looking at things: that the communion with Christ takes place in, and not in spite of, the mess of living. The central character of the story finds himself drawn to, and eventually following, Christ. In so doing he discovers that the stuff of his life—heart-break, poverty, failure—becomes identified for him with the bread of life that Christ takes in his hands and breaks for the life of the world. In this breaking, the young man finds a reflection of his own brokenness. He discovers that the Eucharist is not just something we do, it is something we are; that the body of Christ is not just something we take upon our tongues, but something that together we become.

Like all the stories in this book, *The Perfect Host* explores serious theological questions—not by appealing to the intellect, but by sowing a seed in the imagination. It very much depends on your house group whether they feel able to tackle a discussion of eucharistic theology at an intellectual level. But even if they feel unable to do that, there is no reason why they should not comfortably acquire a conceptual grasp of the issues through reading a story like this.

This story is of medium length and takes about half an hour to read. It *can* be used in a worship context, but it is probably best read in the more comfortable setting of a home meeting. Ideally, this story should be used as a preliminary to your house group discovering the power and beauty of celebrating the Eucharist together as a group.

This might be tackled in two ways. Either the story could be read, and then the Eucharist celebrated straightaway, perhaps using a form of service such as the Iona Community publishes in their worship material; or the story could be read and considered, maybe along the lines suggested below, and then the next meeting could be the occasion of the Eucharist.

If you are celebrating the Eucharist in your house group, do check first with your minister. Some congregations are quite happy for communion to be celebrated without an ordained person present, but elsewhere the conventions may be more rigid. For the sake of peace and good order it is worth respecting the rules of your own denomination.

However, if your priest or minister comes to celebrate communion with your house group, he or she ought to be with you for the whole journey, hearing the story, participating in the study, and consenting to take part as a human being, not as a church official elevated above the others.

In the whole group, read the story.

(35 mins)

Ask the group for their responses to the story, and be prepared for these to be nothing theological whatever—for example, 'I think Trevor and Kathy should have been reunited at the end.'

(10 mins)

If this is not happening already, direct the group now towards thinking about the Eucharist, perhaps by asking them to consider some of these questions (if there are a lot of people in your group, you could split into small groups for this).

- What comes to your mind when somebody uses the phrase 'the body of Christ'?

- Some denominations celebrate communion every day because they see the Eucharist as very special and holy. Some only do so once a year, for the same reason. You are probably somewhere in between, going to a communion service somewhere between once a week and once a month. Is it important to you? How would you describe your experience of Holy Communion?

- Have you ever been part of a Eucharist celebrated in a small home group before? What sort of an experience was that?

- Did you know before you heard the story that in John's Gospel the washing of the feet replaces the institution of the Eucharist? What do you think about that? Why might that be important for us?

- Can you make anything of the thought that suffering, love and Eucharist all have mystery at their heart? That is to say, they touch the hidden heart of God.

(20 mins)

Divide into small groups now if you have not already. In small groups, consider this question:

In the story, Trevor saw the brokenness of his life as being held in the hands of Jesus like the bread broken; like Jesus' body broken. It was something through which goodness and love could flow. Can you think of something that has happened in your life, or a friend's life, where pain and sadness have somehow become a means of grace—a way for goodness to come into people's lives?

(20 mins)

Closing devotions

Join together again as a whole group, and spend a few minutes sharing (or recapping if your group was too small to split) very briefly some of the insights gained from the small group time. These are for leading into worship, not for discussion now, so just a sentence or two from those who want to speak, such as:

- 'I am willing to give God my pain, but I can't see what good can come of it.'
- 'When my mother died, there was this amazing sense of peace and the presence of God.'
- 'How can people believe in God when there is so much suffering?'
- 'In a way, because Jesus suffered, it means we are never alone with our pain.'

If you like, you could read out these thoughts in addition to what the group shares, as examples of what some other people have thought.

Spend a few minutes now in silence.

Prayer

Lord Jesus,
in the time that goes by till we meet again,
prepare us to share in Holy Communion
with each other and with you.
Lead us into the mystery of your sorrow,
your love
and your risen life.
Give us grace to see
beyond what life offers us
the hand that is holding out to us
the gift of today; your hand.
Knowing that you hold our life in your hands,
help us to trust you enough
to abide in the peace of your presence
and believe in your love.
When we lose our way, look for us.
When our courage falters, lift us up.
When our faith is dim, light the way for us.
For you walked this way before us
and you are no stranger in our world.   Amen.

Songs

Lord of the cross of shame
Crown Him with many crowns
Broken for me, broken for you

Share 'the Grace' together.

(20 mins)

Summary

Coffee	15 mins
Story	35 mins
Responses	10 mins
Whole group discussion	20 mins
Small groups	20 mins
Closing devotions	20 mins
Total time	120 mins

Suitable for a 7.30–9.30pm meeting.

Study Notes for A Dream Come True

Ask each person on their own to spend a little while reflecting on the story.

- How does it make you feel?

- Do you feel uncomfortable with the level of hopelessness and despair it expresses?

- Does it make you want to turn away to an easy solution, or to a forgetting of the bleakness and brokenness of the lives in the story?

- How do you personally deal with doubt and despair?

(5 mins)

In groups of two or three, consider one or more of the following questions:

- Do you personally know anyone like the people in this story?

- Imagine you are sitting in a pub with Frank Marsden, and he had just told you this story. What do you think you would say to him?

- If you look around you, you will see a great many people

like Danny Ludlow and his wife and children. Is there anyone in your church who reminds you of them?

(a) If 'yes', what has your church community done to help nurture Danny's faith, and help him to live out his vision of loving family life?

(b) If 'no', why is it, do you think, that people like Danny don't find their way into your church community, even though, like you, they may believe in Jesus?

• In the story, Frank Marsden cared very much about Danny, and responded to him sensitively and with compassion. Do you think it is possible for people like Frank, who themselves cannot believe, to do the work of Jesus?

• Frank was also very ashamed of his own failings, but felt helpless to do anything about them. How did you feel about Frank? How would you feel about helping Frank to accept himself and find healing for the pain that always erupted in violence? Would you feel it was necessary for him to become a Christian to do that?

• Was Danny's faith a genuine faith? Were his ambitions realistic?

• If Danny had had Christian friends who stuck by him, do you think the outcome would have been different for his life and Frank's ability to believe?

(20 mins)

Closing devotions

Readings

Here are some Bible passages to look at together. (It would be helpful if the leader has chosen and reflected on one or two of these beforehand and considered their relationship to the story.)

Matthew 22:28-32
Matthew 18:5-7
Matthew 25:31-46 (NB, there is no reference to religious
   belief in this passage)
Luke 14:34-15:7
Luke 19:10

(20 mins)

Suggestions for prayers

1. A prayer of repentance on behalf of the whole church, for having failed the lost and the wounded, for having neglected the mission of Jesus to seek and to save.
2. A prayer of repentance for the times we have given in to the temptation to make the church into our private club, forgetting that we are servants, not masters.
3. A prayer asking God to give us another chance, to send to us his *anawim* (a Hebrew word, meaning 'God's little ones', the poor and outcast who are precious to him), to give us another opportunity to seek the face of Christ in his broken, suffering ones.

A time for silent reflection.

Song

O Lord hear my prayer (Taizé)

(15 mins)

Summary

Coffee	20 mins
Story	40 mins approx

Reflection alone	5 mins
Small group work	20 mins
Bible study	20 mins
Prayer	15 mins
Total time	120 mins approx

Suitable for a 7.30—9.30pm meeting.

Study Notes for An Invisible Woman

Ask each person on their own to take a few minutes to think back over the story.

- What was the feeling it left you with?

- Does it remind you of anyone you know?

(5 mins)

In small groups consider some of the following. Take your time—you don't need to cover them all.

- Is there anything you want to share from your few minutes thinking quietly on your own?

- Some people, particularly women, feel trapped by the parts they have to play in life: someone's mother, someone's daughter, someone's wife. They long for friends who will see them, love them, for themselves. Is this feeling something you can identify with? What do you think about it?

- Sometimes those who have no voice or authority in society—little children, people with learning difficulties, those who have rejected conventional lifestyles—can offer us insights we might otherwise miss. If we are to become whole people ourselves, we need to listen to the insights of such people, and learn from their different perspectives. What do you think?

- It is easy for a husband and wife to slip into traditional roles. Although this can seem convenient, it actually denies both of them the opportunity to be a fully alive, fully responsible human being. From time to time we could be helped by looking carefully at our relationships, asking ourselves if they reflect Jesus' gift of 'abundant life', or if they look more like the script of a rather predictable play.

(20–25 mins)

Return to the full group, and ask a representative from each small group to give some feedback from the discussion to the whole group. If your group is too small to split up, then look together at the following Bible passages (the leader should have read through these beforehand and reflected on their relevance to the story):

    Psalm 138:1-17
    Luke 10:21-22
    Luke 18:15-17
    Luke 19:1-10
    John 4:5-10, 25-27

(15–20 mins)

Closing devotions

Sit quietly for a few moments, thinking over the time you have spent together, the ideas you have shared and the story you have explored.

Think about the way the attitudes of Jesus challenge us to really see . . . to really listen . . . to really live . . . to really love.

Prayer

Loving God, help us to trust you.
Help us to permit you to draw us out of the prisons we
have built for ourselves, the unlocked prisons in which we
hide.
Help us to come out as we really are,
and to accept each other as we really are,
and to offer each other the joy and the dignity
and the freedom of being loved, just as we are.   Amen.

Readings

'. . . where the Spirit of the Lord is, there is freedom' (2 Cor
3:17).

'And leaving the crowd behind, they took him, just as he
was, in the boat' (Mk 4:36).

Prayer

Just as we are, we invite you, Lord Jesus
to come into the boat with us, just as you are.
Travel with us
adventure with us.
Leave the safety of the harbour and the shore with us.
Let the wind of your Spirit blow
to set us free.   Amen.

Songs

Spirit of the living God, fall afresh on me
Jesus take me as I am
Just as I am without one plea
One more step along the world I go

(15 mins approx)

Summary

Coffee	15 mins
Story	45 mins
Reflection alone	5 mins
Small group work	20–25 mins
Feedback/Bible study	15–20 mins
Closing devotions	15 mins approx
Total time	115–125 mins

Suitable for either a 7.30–9.3pm meeting or, with this particular story, a women's afternoon meeting, or young mothers' group.

Study Notes for Sam in Love

(Pencils and paper will be needed for this session.)

Sam in Love follows on from *An Invisible Woman*, and in some ways they form a pair of stories. It is important to read *An Invisible Woman* first, because familiarity with the main characters is assumed in *Sam in Love*.

This is one of the longest stories in the book, and is intended to be read alone by members of the group, or read aloud in serial form over some weeks. If it is to be serialised, probably the most sensible thing is to break it down into fifteen- or twenty-minute sections, making it a minor part of the meeting (perhaps at the end). When the final part is reached, it could begin the meeting, which could then follow a format such as the one suggested in the notes below.

Read the last episode of the story (if you have been reading it as a serial).

(20 mins)

Ask the whole group to sit quietly and think back over the story.

One of the questions the story *Sam in Love* offers us is:

241

'What kind of God is God?' Get people to ask themselves now: 'What kind of God do I believe in?' (Leave a pause to let people think, then thoughtfully and slowly add some more questions.)

- Do I trust that God?

- Does that God care about me?

- Does that God see me and know me?

- What is my God like?

Give people space and peace to think, then invite those who want to to share the thoughts that have come to them. Be sensitive, leaving space, and if need be giving gentle encouragement for the shyer people to speak if they wish. If you have someone in your group who just loves to bare their soul at every opportunity, work out some strategy for restraining them, such as saying quickly when they draw breath to begin another paragraph, 'Thank you for sharing that. I could really identify with your feelings about your father/dog/teddy bear/bank manager. I wonder if someone who hasn't spoken yet has something they'd like to share?'

(15 mins)

In small groups, spend some time talking about prayer. In the story, Sam and Rosemary ask God to bring about something very specific. Sam wanted to kiss Eleanor, and asked God to fix it so he could. What do you think about this kind of prayer? Is it right to ask God to alter the course of events for us—to find a parking space, to heal a relationship, to help us find our lost car keys? Or is prayer more a case of the way Maxwell saw it, an aligning of our will with God's will? Chew over these thoughts, using the story to help you. Share your ideas with each other.

(20 mins)

Now, still in small groups, ask each person to write a prayer expressing what their essential self is saying to God right now. Emphasise that it should not be a prayer saying what they *think* they should say to the sort of God they've been taught to believe in, but the truth of what their heart wants to say to the God they really believe in.

It might be: 'I am afraid of you, God. You ask too much. I'm not good enough.' Or: 'Why did you let Jack die?' Or: 'Thank you, thank you, thank you for the way things worked out this morning.' Or: 'Here I am, waiting for you. I don't know what to say. I'm not sure who you are, but here I am. Make yourself real for me, if you are there.'

(5 mins)

Invite people to share within their small group what they have written if they want to. Let them talk about what this may have turned up for them.

(10 mins)

Back in the whole group, consider the two ways in which *Sam in Love* looks at our relationships with other people as well as our relationship with God.

1. The story explores the pain and necessity of being vulnerable and honest with our friends, trusting those who are close to us. An example of this is the conversation Sam has with Rosemary when he visits her house to ask for a bath.

2. The story looks at our relationships with people who are very different from us, whose lives and appearances feel strange and frightening. One example is Eleanor's thoughts about the people at the snack bar, as she and Sam walk along the seafront to Sam's flat after the play. Another example is the way Sam's confidence is so undermined by entering Rosemary's clean, respectable home.

Invite the group to share experiences of times when they have been among people who felt different from themselves. Was it exciting? Threatening? Frightening? Interesting?

Ask the group to consider their circle of friends. Do they all tend to be the same kind of people, or are they a very mixed bunch?

(20 mins)

In the whole group, think about some of the people Jesus spent time with. If you did not read an episode of the story, look up the Bible references. If you did, there will not be enough time to do this, so just refer to them.

In addition to those the group think of, here are some of Jesus' friends you might remember:

- *Mary of Bethany*, who seems to have been a prostitute, or at any rate a promiscuous person. Jesus often popped into her home (Lk 7:36–50; Jn 11:1–5;12:1–3).

- *Zaccheus*, a dwarf. Everyone hated him because he was a dishonest and unscrupulous tax collector. His story is laden with loneliness. He made a friend when Jesus invited himself to his place for tea (Lk 19:1–10).

- *Simon the Leper*, a Pharisee. He lived in the same village as Mary of Bethany, but didn't think much of her. He liked to have Jesus at his dinner table as a guest celebrity (Mt 26:6; Mk 14:3; Lk 7:36–45).

- *Simon Peter*, passionate, emotional fisherman. He loved Jesus with every fibre of his being, but disowned him out of sheer terror when Jesus was on trial (Mk 14:29–31, 66–72; Jn 21:15–17).

- *Judas Iscariot*, thief. At the last meal they shared together, a Passover meal, the time came at the end of the meal for the host (Jesus) to offer the sop of bread dipped in wine to the most honoured guest at the table. He gave it to Judas, who stood most in need of his love that night (Jn 12:4–6; 13:26–30).

Spend a few moments considering what Jesus' choice of friends tells us about him. Explore a little the influence of trust and fear on our choices of friends and acquaintances, and on the choices Jesus made.

(20 mins without looking up quotations, 35 mins if doing so)

Closing devotions

Begin with a moment of silence.

Songs

As we are gathered, Jesus is here
There's a quiet understanding
I come before the presence of the Lord God of hosts

Reading

'To you, O Lord, I lift up my soul.
O my God, I rely on you;
do not let me be shamed . . .
Make your ways known to me,
teach me your paths.
Set me in the way of your truth, and teach me,
for you are the God who saves me.
All day long I hope in you' (Ps 25:1–2,4–5).

Prayer

God of life and love, God of laughter and tears,
we have looked at the stories of Jesus,

and there found reflected your face.
The trust, the generosity, the honesty and the kindness
that radiate from the life of Jesus,
show up our narrow-mindedness, our fearfulness, our
snobbery.
Living God, whatever else you do with us,
teach us to trust,
to tell the truth
and to love,
so that our lives will not have been wasted. Amen.

Sing 'Let the beauty of Jesus be seen in me'.
Share together a sign of peace.

(10 mins)

Summary

Coffee	15 mins
(Story	20 mins)
Whole group	15 mins
Small groups 20	
5	
10	35 mins
Whole group	20 mins
Bible study	40 or 20 mins
Devotions	10 mins
Total time	135–155 mins

Suitable for a 7.30–9.45pm meeting.

There is a lot of material to cover in this study. This is
because it touches on some quite intimate things, which
people may not have enough trust in each other to discuss.
If they are not very forthcoming, it is one evening's work.
If they are the sort who find lots to say and share, you may

consider splitting the study material over two evenings, discussing prayer and our relationship with God on one evening, and our relationships with each other at a subsequent meeting. If you decide to do this, and therefore find yourself short of a second set of devotions, try the short piece called *The Dolly* (on page 195) as a meditation to end the session on our relationship with God, and follow it with Psalm 23 or the Lord's Prayer.

Study Notes for A Many Splendoured Thing

Because this is a longer story, the members of the group will either have read it on their own at home, or had it read as a serial to them over two or three weeks. Either way they will have had time to reflect on the story and some of the issues it raises for them.

So first, the leader might offer a brief recap to jog the group's memory, and allow them a period of quietness (up to a minute) to reorientate themselves from the chat of coffee time to the business of the meeting.

It is *strongly recommended* that the leader does *not* at this point ask: 'What did you think of the story?' The reason for this caution is that homosexuality is a subject about which many people have very strong opinions and feelings. To invite general feedback at this stage is to invite your meeting to degenerate into a confusion of prejudice, dimly-remembered quotations from the Bible, hurt feelings and hot air, which is likely to end with a breakdown of communication at around midnight.

If the group feels, having read the story, that it would like to discuss the ethics of homosexual relationships, I would recommend that another date is fixed for this, and that you contact your minister and ask for some guidance with reading, biblical material, and the official stance of your own denomination. The reason for this is (a) homosexuality is such a hot issue and (b) that is not what this story is asking you to look at.

The purpose of this story, rather like Jesus' story of the Good Samaritan, is to help the group explore the love and humanity that the gospel should engender, even between people deeply divided by cultural or ethical beliefs.

Incidentally, an evangelical Christian has criticised this story for giving a gay Christian the last word, rather than leaving the reader with Eric Barton's condemnation of homosexuality ringing in the ears. And a gay Christian has criticised the story for allowing that last word to be so mild in refraining from condemning Eric Barton. (Actually, he said David should have pushed Eric's teeth down his throat!) All of which goes to show that the parable of the Good Samaritan still has much to teach us today.

So, take a deep breath and save the issue of sexual ethics for next week (or later tonight).

(15 mins to explain the above to your house group and look at the possibility of discussing sex some other time.)

With the whole group, read together Luke 10:27–37, the parable of the Good Samaritan. (The leader should read this through properly, aloud, to him or herself the day before the meeting, to let it speak afresh. Don't think that because it is a familiar story there is no need to check it out.)

Direct the attention of the group to the dialogue about the neighbour:

'You shall love your neighbour as yourself.'

'And who is my neighbour?'

'Which of these three, do you think, was neighbour to the man?'

'The one who showed him mercy.'

'Go and do likewise.'

Next, remind the group that in 'passing by on the other side', the priest and the Levite were being well-behaved religious people. To touch someone leaking blood, pus or anything else would have made them ceremonially unclean. This is similar to the outlook of many Christians a generation or so ago (and some even now) who attached a stigma to entering a pub; just to go in made you morally unclean and on the slippery slope to all manner of unimaginable moral decay. Jesus implies that in worrying about their own religious purity, these good people had somehow missed the point.

In other words, the teaching of Jesus in this parable is that the power, the dynamism, of the gospel lies not in defending religious and cultural positions, not in maintaining religious purity, but in trusting God enough to relax and love other people, however different from us their ideas are. We will not catch other people's morals like germs.

Invite comments from the group on this parable.

(20 mins)

Next, invite the group (if it is big enough) to divide into small groups of up to six people, and offer them the following points to think about. They should take their time and choose the things that interest them. They needn't feel obliged to work through them in order.

- In the story, Eric Barton had a really bad time. Do you think he was happy before his wife left, or did the problems start before then? If you think they did, what were his problems really?

- When Amy left, she left a note on the kitchen table to let Eric know. When he wanted Simon to move out, Eric left him a note on the kitchen table to tell him to go. Why do you think they had to leave notes like that, instead of talking face to face? Can you remember times when you had to leave a note because you couldn't face a conversation? Can you talk a little about those times now in the group, and try to understand what was going on inside you and in your relationship with the other person?

• Simon's friend, David, was very angry with Eric, and thought it was unChristian of Eric to throw Simon out. Was he right? What else could Eric have done?

• Imagine for a moment that Eric and Simon were friends of yours, or went to your church. Imagine that it is the week after Simon had moved out. What would you want to say to Eric? How do you think he might be feeling? And what would you want to say to Simon?

(30 mins)

Back in the whole group now, one representative from each group should provide feedback from small-group discussions.

(15 mins)

If the group was too small to split, the leader should recap and draw together the thoughts from the discussion.

(7 mins)

Closing devotions

Start by spending a little while in silence, remembering that you are in the presence of God who loves us, who forgives us, who asks us to love with generosity and with kindness.

(1 min approx)

Reading

'God's gift was not a spirit of timidity, but the Spirit of power, and love, and self-control' (2 Tim 1:7).

The leader should then read the story of *Tulip and the Boating Party*, on page 199.

Prayer

Give us, O living God,
a heart like Jesus
   that sees people's humanity
   that offers healing love
         faithful love.
Give us, O living God,
courage like Jesus
   to speak up for what is right
   to heed the call of the outsider, the lonely, the
     wounded,
   to take risks for the gospel.
Save us, O living God,
   from the imprisonment of the law.
   Set us free: by your grace, set us free.   Amen.

Ask people to open their eyes, look around the room, and ask the question: 'And who is my neighbour?'

(20 mins)

Summary

Coffee	15 mins
Recap on story	3–5 mins
Leader's introduction	15 mins
Bible study	20 mins
Small groups	30 mins

Feedback	7–15 mins
Devotions	20 mins
Total time	110–120 mins

Suitable for an evening meeting with a house group.

(If your group is one that is always saying, 'Oh, don't let's do anything too heavy,' this will either wake them up or make them hate you for ever!)